What Patients and Professionals Are Saying About Doranne Long and *Your Body Book*

Wow, what a book! We both have first-hand experience about how good you are as a Physical Therapist and now we know why. **This book will be invaluable when one gets an injury** and also to prevent it in the first place.

Gene and Nancy Kettwig

For all those who have suffered with pain: you should be so fortunate to have Doranne's experience and healing hands. Her book provides easy-to-follow instructions and suggestions on **how to achieve the relief I found**.

Lanette Mohr-Johns
Hospice Social Worker

Your Body Book is an easy-to-use guide to help improve health and well-being. The book provides basic information on what to do for preventing and managing injury. **An invaluable tool with the overwhelming changes and costs in health care.**

Kay Nielson
Physical Therapy Assistant
Licensed Massage Therapist

Doranne breaks down what is often complex information into a simple, easy-to-understand language. *Your Body Book* is **a great reference book for anyone who has health issues**.

Beth Collins
Founder, *Pain Management through Christ*,
Advocate for those dealing with chronic pain, Fibromyalgia patient

I read *Your Body Book* and loved it! It is accurate and easy to understand! It is **very helpful to anyone interested in helping your body to move more with less stress and pain.** I loved having all of the exercises listed in the back for easy referral. By capturing the specific exercises together, you can follow a program to create health and well-being in your own body. It becomes your own personal educator and trainer. I highly recommend *Your Body Book* to help your body to be working FOR you.

Linda May
Jafra Cosmetics Consultant and Leader

Your Body Book is a well written, easy-to-understand guide to better health. Simple tips and exercises provide the basis for a happier and healthier you.

Carl Sniffen
Attorney, Coach

This delightful and concise little book speaks clearly to the reader (and user). It does not belabor the subject but rather puts useful information readily at the hands of those who will benefit from it.

Kathryn Boranian
Registered Nurse

I appreciate Doranne's heart, soul and spirit as she shares her experience and understanding gained through years of physical therapy practice. I do not hesitate to turn over the care of my patients to Doranne when I am away, fully confident they will be well served. In this user-friendly book she has included information that will be helpful to many, which will accomplish her goal of helping others live higher quality lives.

Don Reordan, PT, MS, OCS, MCTA
Owner of Jacksonville Physical Therapy

How different this book is! One can read and follow the instruction without calling "information." My husband and **I have tried the back exercises — they work!**

Eugenia S. Hagen

I found your book to be well laid out and easy reading. **The illustrations are perfect, easy to follow.** This book is full of useful information. I would purchase a copy and recommend to friends and family.

Susan Blair RN
Riverside Home Health Care

What a great resource! These helpful ideas will allow you to address daily aches and pains or to recover from injury more quickly and successfully.

Mary Collins, MA, CHES
Certified Health Education Specialist

A Head-to-Toe Handbook for Health

YOUR BODY BOOK

Guide to Better Body Motion
with Less Pain

Doranne Long, PT, MS

> This book is intended to provide general health information. Consult qualified professionals with specific health issues.

Copyright © 2011
Doranne Long, PT, MS
All Rights Reserved.

Skellie ™ created by Rose Cassano
Spine © Fotosearch
Cover design – Deborah Perdue

Publisher's Cataloging-in-Publication data

Long, Doranne.
    Your body book: guide to better body motion with less
    pain / Doranne Long
    p. cm.
    Includes glossary and index.
    ISBN 978-0-615-41284-9 (spiral bnd)
    ISBN 978-0-9847077-0-6 (perfect bnd)
    1. Self-care, Health 2. Self-help Techniques.
    3. Pain–Treatment. 4. Exercise Therapy. I. Title.

The Body: Head to Toe, Problems and Solutions, Health Tips,
Exercise

RM 725.L65 2011
615.82-dc22
Library of Congress Control Number: 2010939765

Printed in the U.S.A. by
Morris Publishing®
3212 E. Hwy 30
Kearney, NE 68847

800-650-7888 www.morrispublishing.com

Dedication

This book is dedicated to my parents
who give me roots and wings.
They have always supported me.
They are passionate life-long learners,
as well as writers and editors.
Thank you to my family and friends.
Thank you to all whose paths cross mine
as we learn from each other.

YOUR BODY BOOK

Dem Bones

Ezekiel cried, "Dem dry bones!"
Ezekiel cried, "Dem dry bones!"
Ezekiel cried, "Dem dry bones!"
"Oh, hear the word of the Lord."

The toe bone connected to the
heel bone,
The heel bone connected to the foot bone,
The foot bone connected to the leg bone,
The leg bone connected to the
knee bone,
The knee bone connected to the
thigh bone,
The thigh bone connected to the back bone,
The back bone connected to the neck bone,
The neck bone connected to the head bone,
Oh, hear the word of the Lord!

Dem bones, dem bones gonna walk aroun'
Dem bones, dem bones, gonna walk aroun'
Dem bones, dem bones, gonna walk aroun'
Oh, hear the word of the Lord.

African-American Spiritual Song
Based on Ezekiel 37:1-14

About This Book

The more you know . . .
the better your health and life.

Your Body Book helps you stay healthy and heal when injured or in pain. It provides information about your body, specifically the musculoskeletal system — muscles, bones, and joints.

Not only is "The head bone connected to the neck bone . . ." but every system in the body is interconnected. Your physical body is intimately related to your mental, emotional, and spiritual well-being.

This body book is written for you by an orthopedic manual physical therapist, trained in assessing and treating musculoskeletal problems, with over 30 years of hands-on experience. *Your Body Book* includes a head-to-toe review of the body, identifies problems and solutions to decrease pain and swelling, offers health tips, and recommends exercises to restore motion, improve strength, and promote healing.

This book provides general health information. Consult qualified professionals with specific health issues.

YOUR BODY BOOK

The More You Know

The more you know . . .
the less you have to fear.

The more you know . . .
the better care you can take
of your body.
You can help your body heal.

You will be better able
to control pain,
improve motion and strength.

You will know more
when working with health care
professionals.

The more you know . . .
the more tools you will have
and you will use them well.

TABLE OF CONTENTS

Dedication..vii

Dem Bones ix

About This Book..xi

The More You Know... xiii

I. The Body: Head to Toe................................... 1

Headaches..3

TMJ - Temporomandibular Joint (Jaw)...............4

TMJ Rotation Exercise................................5

Neck (Cervical Spine)..6

Whiplash..8

Neck Care..9

Neck Stretching Exercises......................... 10

Managing Neck Pain 12

Shoulders.. 15

Shoulder Impingement 16

Rotator Cuff Injury.................................... 17

Shoulder Care 18

Shoulder Exercises..................................... 19

Elbow, Wrist, and Hand 24

Mid Back (Thoracic Spine) 25

Thoracic Outlet Syndrome (TOS)................... 26

Ribs.. 27

ɔar Spine) 28

ᴄes 29

.... 30

ain 31

. Pain Relief 32

ᴄk Exercises 33

Pelvis 39

Hips 40

Knees 41

Ankles 42

Feet 44

II. Problems and Solutions 45

Walking When Injured 47

Inflammation 48

-itis (Inflammation) 49

    Arthritis 50

    Bursitis 51

    Tendonitis 52

Noises (Crepitation) 53

Sprain 54

Strain 55

Pain 56

    Pain versus the Problem 57

    The Body Can Lie 58

    Pain Control 59

    Tricking the Body 60

    Goop (Lotion/Gels) 61

Hot or Cold? 62

    Ice Is Nice 64

    Heat 67

Posture/Positioning 68

    Positioning for Pain Relief 70

    Pillows 72

Massage/Manual Therapy 73

III. Health Tips 75

Water 77

Nutrition 78

Sleep 80

Medication 81

Posture 82

Changing Positions 83

Body Mechanics 84

Balance 85

Flexibility 86

Shorter With Age 87

For Women Only: Hormones 88

Weather 89

On the Road Again 90

It's an Emergency! 91

Perspective (Time to Heal) 92

Getting Better 93

Stress 94

Fear 95

Health History/Journal 96

IV. Exercise 97

Exercise 99

Exercise Myths 100

The Body's Rules 101

Rules for Stretching and Strengthening 102

Use It or Lose It 103

Head-to-Toe Exercises 104

TMJ (Jaw) Rotation Exercise 105

Neck Exercises 106

Shoulder Exercises 108

Back Exercises 112

Other Stretching Exercises 118

Closed-Chain Strengthening Exercises 120

Glossary 123

Index 129

About the Author

Contact Information

I. The Body: Head to Toe

A review of dem bones,
their connections,
and how to best care
for muscles, bones, and joints.

Headaches

Muscle tension in the head or neck can cause headaches, which usually start at the base of the skull. As a headache's intensity increases it expands, often to the top or side of the head and behind the eyes.

Treating muscles at the base of the head will often stop headaches. Use ice or heat (see pages 62-67). Apply pressure or massage tight muscles until "it hurts so good," generally for a minute or two.

Two tennis balls, tied tightly in a sock or taped together, can be placed at the base of the head while lying down or leaning against a headrest or wall. Massage the muscles by moving the head on the balls about one inch up and down and/or side to side. This relaxes muscles and stops tension headaches.

There are other *causes* of headaches, in addition to tight muscles at the base of the skull. There are also *different* types of headaches, including migraines. Consult a physician for evaluation.

Tennis Balls

TMJ-Temporomandibular Joint (Jaw)

The jaw joint is a ball and socket with a disc (cushion made of cartilage) between the two bones. Joints should move smoothly, opening and closing without popping, clicking, grinding, uneven motion, or pain. Whiplash or blows to the head can injure the joints, including disc damage or displacement.

Since the jaw is part of the head, and the head bone is connected to the neck bones, it is important to assess the head, neck, jaw, and teeth when there is pain or dysfunction in any of these areas. See specialists with TMJ training — physician, dentist, other dental specialist, or physical therapist.

Normal opening of the mouth should allow three fingers placed sideways between the front teeth. Avoid overstretching (opening the mouth too wide) and creating noise in the joints. Avoid overuse of the jaw joints and muscles by not chewing gum or sticky foods, such as caramels, chewing on only one side of the mouth, or sucking on candy or cigarettes.

To decrease or prevent TMJ problems, teeth should always be slightly separated, not clenched or touching, except when eating. The tongue should rest on the roof of the mouth. This is called the **TMJ resting position**. In addition, TMJ rotation exercises improve health and motion of the joints, and can relieve pain.

TMJ (Jaw) Rotation Exercise

Six repetitions, six times a day.

Most joints are filled with fluid. Motion moves the fluid in joints, providing lubrication and nutrition to bones and cartilage. In jaw joints, motion also helps maintain the disc alignment, mobility, and health.

With the tongue touching the roof of the mouth, open and close the mouth, as is comfortable. This motion should be pain free, symmetrical (the same on both sides), and without crepitation (noise including pops, clicks, and grinding).

This exercise:

- Lubricates the joints and improves circulation
- Decreases pain
- Relaxes muscles
- Improves joint alignment and motion
- May decrease or resolve joint noises
- Is especially beneficial before and after eating, and/or after clenching teeth.

Neck (Cervical Spine)

The spine contains 24 bones (vertebrae); seven cervical vertebrae are in the neck. Each bone has an ideal position creating a natural curve. Joints, connecting bone to bone, allow motion. Each joint should be aligned (in the correct position) and move freely. Muscles balance the head on the neck and provide motion. If any muscle is too tight and strong, or overstretched and weak, the neck may be in dysfunction, resulting in pain, headache, and/or loss of motion.

Between each vertebra is a thin disc (made of cartilage) acting as a cushion. With age, discs become thinner. DDD (degenerative disc disease) is the thinning of discs. With age or injury, the body can develop arthritis (inflammation of a joint). This can cause DJD (degenerative joint disease), boney changes such as bone spurs.

DDD and DJD indicate the spine is getting older, showing some wear and tear. DDD, DJD, or arthritis does not necessarily cause pain. It does mean you need to take good care of your neck by maintaining good posture, mobility of the joints, muscle flexibility, and strength.

YOUR BODY BOOK

Inside the spinal cord are nerves, which connect the body to the brain. They exit the spine through foramen (opening between each vertebra). Nerves from the neck run into the head and down the arms. Nerves can be compressed by bones, discs, swelling, poor posture or positioning. Sensations of pins, needles, tingling, numbness, and/or weakness can be signs of pressure on a nerve (impingement).

The joints (facets), connecting each vertebra, can become pinched and/or inflamed (swollen) causing sharp pain. This can happen simply by "sleeping wrong" and will usually resolve with time.

Necks often lose motion with age or injury. To be safe, a driver needs to turn the head at least 60 degrees, which is 2/3 of the way to the shoulder.

General rules for the neck:

- Pulling sensations indicate the neck is tight, stiff, and needs to be stretched (slowly and gently).
- With sharp pinching pain, be gentle. Avoid motions and/or positions that cause pain.
- A smaller area, or decreased intensity, of pain/ symptoms is good.
- If moving the neck causes pain/symptoms elsewhere in the body, seek medical attention.

Whiplash

Whiplash is a general term used when the neck is snapped quickly; this often occurs in a car accident. Ligaments (connecting bone to bone) may be stretched, facet joints may be compressed, and muscles may become tight and painful.

With a whiplash, seek medical attention and begin treatment, even if you believe you are not injured. Sometimes onset of symptoms occurs later when the body becomes stiff. Use ice immediately after any injury because it will decrease pain, swelling, and muscle spasms (see pages 62-67). The first priority is to decrease pain. Then restore motion and assist the body to heal with good rest and nutrition.

It may take a year to recover completely from a whiplash because ligaments can take that long to heal. Morning stiffness is typical because ligaments become stiff when not moving. Injured muscles fatigue more quickly, often becoming sore as the day progresses. Weather changes (air pressure change) also affect the body, especially when swelling is present. *"I can feel it in my bones; it's going to rain."*

Neck Care

To maintain a healthy neck, it is important the muscles and joints have good flexibility (able to move freely) and be pain free.

The head should sit neutrally on top of the neck; poor posture or positioning can create pain and headaches. With neck pain or headache, use ice, heat or alternate them, whatever feels best. Ice decreases pain, swelling, and muscle spasms. Heat increases blood flow and decreases stiffness (see pages 62-67). Support the neck with a pillow, towel roll, or rice sock (see pages 12-13).

Stretching exercises improve neck motion. The joints will be lubricated and healthier. The muscles will receive better blood flow and be more relaxed. In addition to stretching, strengthening exercises may be indicated.

Neck Stretching Rules

- Pulling/stretching sensations are **OK**.
- Increased motion and/or decreased pain is good.
- Sharp pinching pain is **not OK**.
- Decreased motion, increased pain or other symptom is bad.

Neck Stretching Exercises

Three repetitions, move slowly, hold for three seconds or more, three times a day. Do in the shower, in the car, with a towel or rice sock for support if desired. Keep shoulders down and back.

- **Chin Tuck**. Lower chin about one inch, creating a double chin, to stretch the upper neck muscles at the base of the skull.

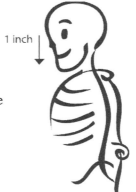

- **Neck Flexion. Chin-to-Chest** to stretch muscles on the back of the neck. Then turn the head to the left and right; this stretches muscles at the base of the skull allowing the head to turn on the first two neck vertebrae. Half of the neck's ability to turn occurs in the upper cervical region.

Neck Stretching Exercises (continued)

Three repetitions, move slowly, hold for three seconds or more, three times a day.

- **Neck Rotation**. Turn head to the left and right. It is important, especially when driving, to be able to turn the head at least 60 degrees, which is 2/3 of the way to the shoulder.

- **Neck Side Bend**. Tilt head to the left and right, moving the ear toward the shoulder, without allowing the head to turn.

- **Do not** tilt the head back if it causes dizziness or light-headedness. Tilting back could decrease the blood flow to the brain, which is not good. If tilting the head back, try supporting the back of the neck with your fingers, a towel, or rice sock (see next page).

Managing Neck Pain

Ice, heat, massage, stretching, and sometimes traction can help manage neck pain. Good posture and avoiding prolonged or awkward positions. Prevent pain and headaches with good posture and avoiding prolonged or awkward positions. Avoid tilting the head back when reaching overhead, in the shower, shaving, applying make-up, or with hair care; use a straw to drink.

Rice Sock. Pour two pounds of uncooked rice in a long sock (tie/sew to close) to create a comfortable neck support. The sock can be heated in a microwave for about two minutes or until comfortably warm. It can also be frozen. The sock should feel good and provide support; use it to assist moving the head and neck. Use day and night as needed.

Support. Neck muscles become fatigued trying to balance the head. A rice sock or towel roll around the neck can decrease strain. To remove the weight of the head from the neck, lie down. Find the best pillow by trial-and-error for comfort and to support the head and neck.

Stretch. The neck moves and feels better after stretching. Stretch while using a heated rice sock or when in the shower or hot tub to warm the tissues, improve motion, and decrease pain.

YOUR BODY BOOK

Massage. Feel for tight muscles on the front, back, sides of the neck, and at the base of the skull. "Hurt so good" massage, strumming, and acupressure (sustained pressure for at least 30 seconds) can be uncomfortable but help relax muscles.

Posture. Bad posture limits neck motion. Good posture decreases neck pain and problems: no *"goose necking,"* keep the chin tucked, head on straight, shoulders back and down. When driving, the back of the head should touch the headrest. Avoid prolonged forward head positions when reading, turned to one side to use the computer, or altered positioning with bi/trifocal glasses and when on the phone.

Position. Neck pain can often be resolved with positioning. If a neck muscle is in spasm, change position so the muscle relaxes, feels soft, and is no longer tender to touch. Remain in that pain-free position for at least 90 seconds. For example, if the tight painful muscle is on the left side of the neck, gently tilt the head to the left; turn the head a little to the left or right depending on which direction relaxes the muscle (see page 70).

Neck Traction. Traction lifts the weight of the head off the neck to relieve pain, decrease pinching, and/or improve motion. A head weighs about 10-12 pounds; gently lifting with hands, a towel, an over-the-door traction, or a mechanical traction unit may provide symptom relief.

Traction should feel good with decreased symptoms afterwards. It is most beneficial when tissue needs to be unpinched. Tight muscles may not appreciate being stretched and could actually become more sore/tight.

Generally, traction is applied:

- Once or twice a day, for about 10 minutes.
- With about 8-10 pounds of pull, more if comfortable, maximum of 20 pounds.
- With a steady or intermittent pull.
- With an over-the-door traction unit, the head can turn while in traction, if it feels good.

Adjust any change in traction carefully. When finishing a treatment, slowly release the pull to avoid sudden compression or muscle spasm.

Consult a health care professional before using traction to see if it is recommended and for specific instructions.

Shoulders

The shoulder joint connects the upper arm bone (humerus) to the shoulder blade (scapula). The shoulder blade connects to the neck and back, as well as to ribs and the collar bone (clavicle), which are connected to the breast bone (sternum). Therefore, shoulder problems can involve other parts of the body and vice versa.

Because the shoulder is a large joint, it "lies." Where the pain is felt is not necessarily where the problem is. Pain is often felt at the top of the shoulder, or a few inches down the arm, but the problem could be in the neck or anywhere in the shoulder area. Shoulder pain usually refers down the arm, the farther down the arm the worse the problem.

Anything that makes the shoulder more comfortable is good; the smaller the area of pain, the better. This includes: shoulder shrugs/circles, lean over and let the arm hang, swing the arm like a pendulum, pull it gently to create traction, vibration, place small towel/pillow between the arm and body or under the arm. Pillows under the arm can assist with sleep. Painful shoulders do not like to be slept on.

Limited motion is usually the reason shoulders hurt. Restoring correct motion will decrease pain and resolve the problem. Stretching, while uncomfortable at the time, will actually help the shoulder feel better.

Shoulder Impingement

Sharp pain with shoulder motion could be an impingement; tissues are pinched and become inflamed (hot, red, swollen, painful).

The space between the bones at the top of the shoulder is less than ¼ inch. When tissues in this space are pinched, sharp pain occurs often with raising the arm to 90 degrees when driving, combing hair, and putting dishes into a cupboard. Avoid sharp pinching pains; use the good arm to assist the other. Avoid aggravating activities; for example, drive with hands low on the steering wheel, rather than at the 10:00 and 2:00 o'clock positions.

Impingement can occur with a fall or overuse of the arm. Additional reasons could be a bone spur or calcium deposits under the acromion (outside part of the shoulder blade at the top of the shoulder). Bursitis occurs when a bursa (sac of fluid) beneath the acromion becomes inflamed (swollen). Ice (see pages 62-67), placed at the top of the shoulder, is helpful to decrease pain and swelling. Bursitis will resolve with time, but an injection into the bursa, usually by an orthopedic surgeon, can quickly reduce the swelling and pain.

Shoulder impingement can also occur when muscles around the shoulder are too tight, not allowing the head of the humerus to move correctly in the socket. Stretching the shoulder can often stop the impingement.

Rotator Cuff Injury

The rotator cuff consists of four muscles. These are the:

- Supraspinatus — above the spine of the scapula (ridge of bone on the shoulder blade)
- Infraspinatus — below the spine of the scapula
- Teres minor — below the infraspinatus
- Subscapularis — under the shoulder blade, next to the ribs

The supraspinatus muscle runs along the top of the shoulder blade, under the acromion, and attaches to the top of the shoulder. This muscle can become pinched or torn. When injured, the shoulder can be very painful especially when trying to lift the arm. The other rotator cuff muscles can also be injured; usually they are tight and painful, but not torn.

The worst case scenario, with a rotator cuff tear, is not being able to lift the arm. The pain can be excruciating, probably radiating down the entire arm. The shoulder will be painful at night; try resting in a recliner with the arm supported on pillows. Ice (see pages 62-67), hot showers, TENS (transcutaneous electrical nerve stimulation, see page 60), medications, and physical therapy may be helpful. If the shoulder is not getting better, consult an orthopedic surgeon.

Shoulder Care

Most shoulder problems are fixable. Whatever decreases the intensity of the pain, or results in a smaller area of pain, is good. Use ice, especially with acute, sharp pinching pain. Use heat to warm tight tissues, if it feels good. Rice socks, hot showers, hot tubs, and exercise are all helpful in warming the shoulder. Stretching can be uncomfortable but is necessary to restore range of motion (ROM) to shoulders.

Because muscles hold the ball in the socket, any muscle that is too tight, weak, and/or painful will affect the alignment of the shoulder. The shoulder needs to be positioned correctly to function well. Keeping the shoulders back with good posture helps better align the ball in the socket.

A painful shoulder is almost always a tight shoulder. Most problems resolve with restored motion. First, restore motion; then strengthen the muscles. Find tight and sore muscles around the shoulder, including in front and back of the axilla (armpit); massage or place pressure on the sore spots for about 30 seconds. This helps muscles relax and allows for improved motion, even though "it hurts so good."

Shoulder Exercises

Shoulder stretching exercises

Ten repetitions, hold at least ten seconds, at least two to three times a day.

Stretching can be uncomfortable, but if the motion improves, keep going. Stretching pain is OK. Avoid sharp pinching pain. When the shoulder becomes more sore, or starts to lose motion, stop!

Shoulders often become painful because of limited motion. This can occur:

- When a muscle spasms following a quick motion such as catching a tipping glass.

- With inactivity; only about 50% of full motion is needed for normal life activities, such as combing hair, reaching, and dressing.

- With poor posture; forward shoulders limit shoulder (and neck) motion.

The goal of stretching is to increase motion. Shoulders are large joints, and usually require aggressive stretching.

Rotation exercises spin the ball in the socket, which stretches the joint and allows better motion. Better shoulder external and internal rotation also improves shoulder flexion (reaching overhead).

Shoulder stretching — external rotation

Ten repetitions, hold at least ten seconds, at least three times a day.

Stretching can be uncomfortable, but if the motion improves, keep going. Stop when motion decreases or the shoulder becomes more sore.

Improved external rotation (needed to throw a ball) may resolve an impingement in the shoulder, often caused by tightness in the subscapularis and pectoral muscles. Improved shoulder rotation also improves reaching overhead.

- **"ER-at-side."** Elbows at the side of the body, elbows bent 90 degrees, move hands away from the stomach. This exercise stretches the subscapularis muscle, which is under the shoulder blade.

- **"Stick-em-up."** With arms elevated to 90 degrees away from the side of the body, elbows bent 90 degrees, move arms back. This stretches a large chest muscle (pectoralis major) and a smaller muscle (pectoralis minor).

These exercises can be done lying, sitting, standing, in the shower, walking, or stretching in a doorway.

Shoulder stretching — *internal rotation*

Ten repetitions, at least three times a day.

Stretching can be uncomfortable, but if the motion improves, keep going. Stop when motion decreases or the shoulder becomes more sore.

To improve internal rotation, stretch by reaching behind the back. The goal is for both hands to touch the same place in the back. Women can usually reach their bra strap; men need to reach their back pocket. Improved internal rotation allows for better overall shoulder motion, including reaching overhead.

- **"Chicken wings."** With hands at the waist, or behind the back, move elbows forward and backward. Move only the elbows; do not allow the shoulder blades to move.

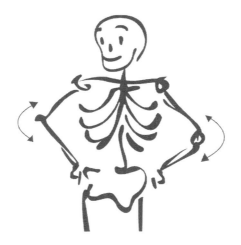

Shoulder stretching — flexion

Ten repetitions, hold at least ten seconds, at least three times a day.

Stretching can be uncomfortable, but if the motion improves, keep going. Stop when motion decreases or the shoulder becomes more sore. Avoid sharp pinching pain, which usually occurs around 90 degrees elevation.

Flexion is reaching overhead. When lying on the back, the arms will ideally reach overhead and rest on the ground/bed, with elbows straight, next to the ears. With age, shoulders may lose some motion but the arms should go back at least next to the eyes for functional motion.

Stretching can be done lying, sitting, standing, in a doorway, or bending forward with hands on a counter/railing. It can be painful to bring the arm down. Move the arm slowly and avoid sharp painful positions. Use the "good" arm to assist the "bad" arm.

Shoulder strengthening exercises

Once a day, pain free, to fatigue, goal of 30 repetitions. Move smoothly; the slower the better, especially upon release.

More repetitions increase strength. However, exercise only to fatigue. Muscles will not become stronger if there is pain.

Muscles need 24 hours to recover from a workout; continuing to exercise or work after the muscles become tired could cause further injury and actually slow down healing.

Strengthening exercises include using: exercise equipment, free weights, resistance bands, and doing push-ups against the wall/counter, or on the floor. It is important to strengthen the four small rotator cuff muscles. These exercises are especially beneficial:

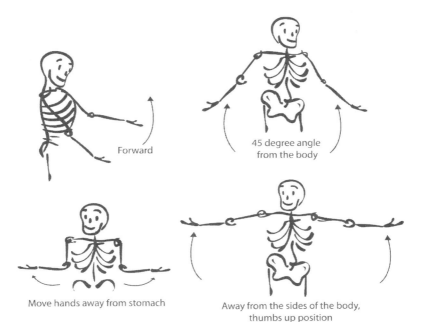

Forward

45 degree angle from the body

Move hands away from stomach

Away from the sides of the body, thumbs up position

Elbow, Wrist, and Hand

Tendonitis (inflammation of a tendon) is common from overusing the arms. For example:

- "Tennis elbow" (lateral epicondylitis) on the outside of the elbow
- "Golfer's elbow" (medial epicondylitis) on the inside of the elbow

-itis means inflammation, resulting in heat, redness, swelling, and pain. Ice is beneficial with any acute injury or inflammation. See chapters on tendonitis and icing.

Avoid painful and repetitive activities. Take frequent breaks, even for just 30 seconds, every 10 minutes. Adjust positions and postures frequently. Use braces or splints. Certified Hand Therapists (CHT), either occupational or physical therapists, are experts for upper extremity (arm) problems.

Mid Back (Thoracic Spine)

In the spine, below the seven neck vertebrae, are 12 thoracic vertebrae. A pair of ribs attaches to each thoracic bone. Ribs can shift out of position. When this occurs, sharp pain can result, especially with breathing. The pain can wrap around and/or shoot through the chest. Pain with breathing is a clue to a rib problem.

The first rib is located a few inches toward the shoulder from the base of the neck. An elevated first rib can put pressure on the arteries, veins, and nerves in the area, leading to a variety of symptoms affecting the arm and/or neck.

Poor posture and/or working in a flexed position (e.g. bent forward over a counter) for a prolonged time can cause back pain. Stand erect, put one foot up on a stool, change positions, and take stretching breaks (see page 36) frequently, to avoid or resolve pain.

See pages 26-27 and page 87 for additional information. Consult a health care professional for evaluation and treatment of an elevated first rib and other thoracic conditions involving the vertebrae and/or ribs.

Thoracic Outlet Syndrome (TOS)

Nerves from the neck run under the collar bone (clavicle), through the arm pit (axilla) and into the arm. Pressure on arteries, nerves, and veins in the collar bone area, causing numbness, pain, and/or decreased circulation, is called thoracic outlet syndrome (TOS). Symptoms are often felt in the arm when it is raised or while sleeping in a curled position.

Avoid aggravating postures and positions; use pillows to prevent pressure on nerves. Good posture and stretching can help, especially the neck, shoulder, and chest muscles, including the pectoral muscles (see page 20). The specific cause and therefore treatment is varied; consult a health care professional for assessment and treatment of thoracic outlet syndrome.

Ribs

A pair of ribs attaches to each of the 12 thoracic vertebrae and wraps around the chest to connect to the sternum (breast bone). The first rib is located a few inches toward the shoulder from the base of the neck. See pages 25-26.

Ribs can shift out of position, which can cause pain usually felt in between the shoulder blades. The pain can be very sharp and can wrap around or shoot through the chest. It hurts to breathe.

With rib pain, try ice to numb the pain and relax the muscles. A hot bath may help. Find a pain-free position, usually bending forward or to one side. See pages 62-67 and page 70 for additional information.

To return a rib to its normal position, try putting pressure on the rib (the rib feels hard like a knuckle), usually between the shoulder blades and the spine, using: a tennis ball, foam roll, or therapy ball, leaning against the corner of a door frame, or backward over a chair. An elevated first rib can be pushed down toward the toes, while exhaling (blowing out air); repeat three times.

These techniques can be uncomfortable. However, once the correct rib position is restored, the sharp pain stops and breathing should be pain free.

Low Back (Lumbar Spine)

The low back has five bones (lumbar vertebrae), labeled L1 through L5 from the top down. L5 is connected to the sacrum (triangle bone at the base of the spine). The coccyx (tail bone) is at the tip of the sacrum.

Between each vertebra is a disc (made of cartilage) that provides cushioning and absorbs shock. With age or injury, the disc becomes thinner, which can lead to DDD (degenerative disc disease). Discs feel little pain; disc problems do not necessarily create back pain.

Bones age, and/or become injured, which can lead to DJD (degenerative joint disease). This may not cause pain, but does show wear and tear.

Disc Injuries

The disc between each bone (vertebra) acts as a cushion and shock absorber. The low back discs are about ¼ inch thick. The outside of the disc is hard; the inside (nucleus) is more jelly-like. Cracks in the outer ring and/or disc bulges can occur. If the damage is severe, the nucleus pushes out resulting in a herniated disc. Disc damage may not be painful; pain occurs when pressure is placed on a nerve.

Herniated discs tend to occur with heavy lifting or working in a forward-bent position. Men, between the ages of 20-40 performing manual labor, are more prone to disc injuries. Coughing, sneezing, straining, and sitting increase pressure on nerves and create more pain.

Sitting is especially painful with disc problems because it increases pressure on discs. While sitting, disc material may ooze out, putting more pressure on nerves causing excruciating pain. **Avoid sitting!** Sit a maximum of 20 minutes at a time, if pain free. Use a lumbar support cushion/rolled towel in the small of the back to keep the natural curve. After sitting, stand tall; do several back bends to restore the curve in the low back. See pages 35-36 for back extension exercises.

Backs are stiffer in the morning especially with a disc problem. Because discs swell when asleep, there is more pressure on the nerves when awakening. Do not bend forward; if necessary, lie on the bed to dress. Walk or stand for about an hour to allow the disc pressure to decrease; avoid sitting, especially on the toilet. Avoid constipation; talk to a doctor for assistance.

Stenosis (Narrowing)

With age, discs become harder and thinner, which result in a person becoming shorter. Backs over 40 years of age tend not to have acute disc injuries but rather DDD (degenerative disc disease) or stenosis (narrowing) of the spinal canal. Symptoms of stenosis include: (a) pain when walking but not sitting and (b) less pain when bending forward, using a walker or pushing a grocery cart. If nerves are compressed because vertebrae are too close together, the body naturally adjusts. Sitting or bending forward opens the back of the spine and decompresses nerves. Flexion exercises may be helpful, including pelvic tilts and knee-to-chest stretching (see pages 33-34). Consult a health care practitioner for further assessment.

Back Pain

Low back pain can result from a variety of problems:

- Pressure on a nerve, from disc bulges, boney changes, or swelling (inflammation)
- A joint (facet) could be swollen (inflamed), arthritic, or unable to move properly (stuck open or closed)
- Tight muscles including the psoas, which attaches to the front of the low back vertebrae and runs through the groin to the front of the hip
- SIJ (sacro-iliac joint) dysfunction; the joint could be out of alignment or not moving properly

Keys to resolving back pain are to:

- Decrease pain with ice, heat, and positioning
- Restore correct alignment (position) of bones and joints
- Restore motion
- Strengthen back and stomach muscles, including the deep core muscles
- Use good posture and body mechanics to prevent re-injury
- Give the body time to heal

Back Pain Relief

Anything increasing the **frequency, intensity, duration,** or **area** (**FIDA**) of back pain or other symptoms such as pins/needles and numbness is bad. Pain or other symptoms referring into the legs is bad; the farther down the leg, the worse the problem. Loss of bowel or bladder control, or the use of a leg, is an emergency. See a doctor immediately!

The goal is smaller/centralized pain into the low back. Use ice for muscle spasms and/or acute pain (where pain is 5 to 10 on a scale of 10). Use heat when the pain is less than 5 and the back is more stiff than painful. Pools and hot tubs create a more weightless environment and allow for more motion and relaxation.

The most relaxing position is lying on the back, with the legs supported on pillows, couch, or chair. If the knees are slightly separated (frog leg), the buttock muscles can relax even more. In addition, try placing a rolled towel in the small of the back. Lying on one side is usually comfortable; place a pillow between the legs to decrease strain to the back, pelvis, hips, and legs. Use lots of pillows to position comfortably. Sleeping on the stomach is not recommended.

For additional information, see pages 62-67 and pages 70-72.

Back Exercises

These exercises are to be done gently and should help the back feel better. Generally start with stretching, then progress to pain-free strengthening.

Back flexion exercises flatten the back, open the joints of the spine, and stretch muscles.

Three to ten repetitions, hold three to ten seconds, one to three times a day, as needed. Lie on the back (on bed/floor) with knees bent.

- **Pelvic tilts**. Press low back to the floor by tightening the stomach muscles. This stretches, strengthens, and lubricates the low back. Pelvic tilts can also be performed when sitting or standing.

- **Knee-to-chest stretching**. Bring one or both knees toward the chest stretching the low back and buttock muscles. If this feels good, and the back feels better afterwards, it is a good exercise.

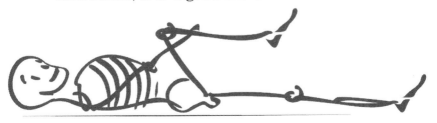

Back flexion strengthening exercises

Build up to 30 times, once a day; must be pain free. Lie on the back (on bed/floor) with knees bent. Move smoothly, the slower the better, especially upon release.

- **Curl-ups**. **Crunches**, not full sit-ups. Lift head and shoulders, tightening stomach muscles, but do not involve the legs. Arms can be placed across the chest, along the side of the body, behind the head or pointed to the ceiling.

- **Bridges**. Lift hips a few inches. This strengthens the back, buttock, and leg muscles.

Back extension stretching exercises

These increase the curve of the low back. They can be especially beneficial to decrease pressure on nerves causing back and/or leg symptoms, often present with a disc injury. The goal is centralized (smaller) symptoms in the back and legs. Do as often as needed to decrease symptoms (on bed/floor).

- **Prone-on-elbows**. Up to several minutes, as is comfortable. Lie on stomach; prop up on elbows, with low back relaxed in a swayed-back position.

- **Press-up**. Three to ten repetitions, as needed, if increased motion and decreased/centralized symptoms. Lie on stomach, propped on elbows; then straighten elbows, keeping the pelvis on the floor, to increase the arch in the low back.

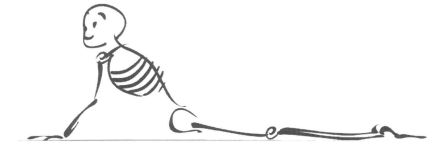

Back extension exercises (continued)

- **Back bends standing**. Three to ten repetitions, as it feels good, with increased motion and decreased symptoms, as often as needed. Hands, or a towel, for support in the small of the back can help. Look straight ahead; the head should not tilt back. This exercise is especially good after sitting or bending forward.

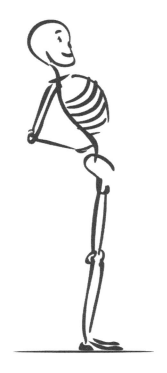

Sometimes tight hip or buttock muscles can cause back pain. This includes the psoas muscle, which attaches to the front of the low back vertebrae and runs through the groin to the front of the hip.

Prone knee flexion/hip rotation stretching exercises.

Three to ten repetitions, **once or twice a day**, as needed with the goal of good motion (same on each side) and symptom relief. These can be done on the bed/floor, or standing, holding onto a counter/railing, without pain, back or pelvic motion.

- **Prone knee flexion stretching**. Lie on stomach; bend one knee to stretch the front thigh muscles. Ideally, the heel should be about six inches from the buttock.

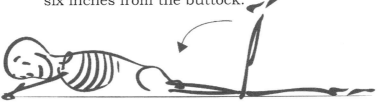

- **Prone hip rotation stretching**. Lie on stomach; bend one knee to 90 degrees, then move that lower leg to the left and right to stretch the hip joint and buttock muscles.

Back Strengthening Exercises

Back exercises should include strengthening the abdominal muscles along with *core strengthening* of the deep back/pelvic muscles. Strengthening exercises must be pain free. Perform them smoothly; the slower the better, especially upon release. Generally, strengthening exercises are performed once a day, 10 to 30 repetitions, increasing the number as able. Basic strengthening exercises include:

- **Pelvic Tilts.** See page 33.
- **Curl-ups/crunches.** See page 34.
- **Bridges.** See page 34.
- **Arm and leg lifts,** while lying on stomach or back.

A therapy ball and/or foam roll can be used for strengthening and balance.

Pelvis

The pelvis consists of the sacrum, the triangle bone at the base of the spine, and the ilium, the large pelvic bone on each side. The pelvis is connected at the front in the pubic area. A sacro-iliac (SI) joint connects the sacrum to each ilium at the back of the pelvis. The SI joints can shift out of alignment, get stuck, and/or not move correctly. The ilium and sacrum can slip up or down, tilt, and/or rotate forward or backward causing back, pelvic, or leg pain and/or other symptoms.

The part of the body that is not moving correctly may not be painful. However, other compensating tissues may be moving too much and then become painful. For example, the right sacro-iliac joint (SIJ) may be stuck, but the pain may be felt in the left SIJ or buttock region. See the next page for additional information about hip, groin, and buttock pain.

It is important to have the back and pelvis assessed by a health care professional, with specific attention to the alignment and motion of the SI joints.

Hips

The hip joint is large and includes the ball, which is the head of the femur (thigh bone), and the socket (acetabulum). Arthritis (DJD) of the hip may cause *groin pain*, loss of motion, and usually pain when bearing weight. Water exercises place the hip in a weightless environment and can help. Use a cane on the opposite side to decrease weight on the painful leg (see pages 47 and 83).

Groin pain can also result from problems in muscles running down the front of the hip such as the psoas muscle and other hip flexors that bend the hip, or the inner thigh muscles that attach to the pubic bone at the front of the pelvis.

Buttock pain can be caused by a variety of problems in the back, sacro-iliac joints (SIJ), or with tight muscles, trigger points, or bursitis. A thorough evaluation is necessary of the back, pelvic alignment, hip motion, and lower extremity flexibility including the ilio-tibial band (ITB), which is very thick tissue that runs down the outside of the thigh.

See page 33 for knee-to-chest stretching exercise. See page 37 for hip flexor and rotator muscles stretching exercises.

Knees

The knee joint includes the thigh bone (femur) and the shin bone (tibia). The fibula is the small bone on the outside of the lower leg. The knee is a hinge joint; it bends and straightens. However, there is some side-to-side and rotation movement. Ligaments (connecting bone to bone) provide stability for the knee by preventing excessive motion. The knee cap (patella) is a floating bone that glides through a groove in the femur.

Pain and swelling in front of the knee usually indicates a knee cap problem. Chondromalacia (softening of patellar cartilage) means the under surface of the knee cap has been damaged and is becoming rough. There may be grinding but not necessarily pain.

Pain on either side of the knee could indicate a ligament sprain or a problem inside the joint. Pain behind the knee usually indicates swelling in the joint.

Meniscus (C-shaped cartilage in the knee) provides cushioning between the femur and tibia. Menisci (one medial and one lateral) can be injured particularly when compressed and twisted. When torn, they can catch and cause the knee to give way. They have poor circulation and may not heal when injured. Surgery can repair or remove an injured meniscus.

For additional information and exercises, see pages 43-44, 47, 50, 53, 60, 62-67, 72, 80, 82, 85, 90, 112-113, 116, 118-120.

Ankles

Sprained ankles occur frequently; usually the foot twists suddenly and ligaments are overly stretched. If swelling occurs immediately, blood vessels have been broken and there will be bruising. Apply ice and compression immediately to decrease bleeding into the tissues.

Rest, **Ice**, **Compress**, and **Elevate** (**R.I.C.E.**) the ankle. Because the body responds to injury with pain and swelling, ice is best. Wrap the ankle with an elastic bandage to decrease swelling and to provide support; use a brace if needed. If painful to bear weight, crutches would be advised.

To rehabilitate an ankle sprain:

- Ice immediately (see pages 62-67).

- Use heat and warm baths when the ankle is no longer hot to touch and more stiff than painful.

- Restore motion with gentle exercises; move the foot up, down, and side-to-side. See page 119 for calf muscles stretching.

- Resume walking as able; use a crutch or cane on the opposite side of the injured leg (see page 47).

- Do **pain-free** strengthening and balance activities: use a resistance band, toe tap, walk on toes, walk on heels, stand on one leg.

- Return to normal activities, gradually, pain free, and without increased swelling.

YOUR BODY BOOK

If there is persistent swelling, elevate the leg when able, ideally above the heart. Gently massage and stroke, pushing the fluid toward the heart. Wear compression stockings or ankle brace to prevent additional swelling. Do ankle pumps — move foot up and down — to push fluid with muscle contractions.

Ligaments (connecting bone to bone) can take a year to heal completely. They are not very elastic and have a poor blood supply. Once injured, they may never fully recover, and may be unable to perform their function of providing stability to joints. They tend to become stiff and sore when immobile and with weather changes. In addition, muscles and tendons, along with arteries, nerves, and veins, can be injured and take time to heal.

Ankle disorders may need to be evaluated by specialists. A thorough evaluation should include assessment of the: back, pelvis, hips, knees, ankles, and feet. Back pain can refer symptoms down the legs. Tightness in the hips or buttocks affects the knees, ankles, and feet. If the pelvis is not aligned correctly, legs can be of different lengths; this affects other joints.

Feet

Plantar fasciitis (inflammation of the thick fascial tissue along the bottom of the foot) is painful. Symptoms include excruciating pain after sitting and when getting out of bed because the tissues are stretched after being relaxed. Plantar fasciitis usually goes away with time, but there are things to try to resolve the problem:

- **Ice**. Three to five times a day (see pages 62-67). A frozen water bottle can be rolled under the foot.

- **Stretch**. Stretch the plantar fascia and calf muscles, especially before getting out of bed and after sitting; move feet up and down. Stretch the calf muscles (see page 119):
  - Gastrocnemius muscle, with the knee straight.
  - Soleus muscle, with the knee bent.
- **Physical therapists and podiatrists** can help; **orthotics (shoe inserts)** may be indicated.

Many people have arthritis in their feet, usually in the toes, similar to their hands. Arthritis tends to be inherited; but does not necessarily cause pain. Feet disorders may need to be evaluated by specialists. The back, pelvis, hips, knees, ankles, and feet all need to be assessed at the time of the evaluation.

II. Problems and Solutions

Problems with the
musculoskeletal system
— muscles, bones, and joints —
are generally fixable
and will heal with time.
The healing process can be
less painful and more successful
when you work with your body.

Decrease pain and swelling,
correct alignment,
restore motion,
then proceed with
pain-free strengthening.

Walking When Injured

When walking, arms swing opposite to the legs. Therefore, use a cane or crutch on the other side of the painful leg.

- The cane, crutch, or walker moves first, then the injured leg, and then the other leg. Or, the painful leg moves forward with the walking aid.
- The **good** leg goes first **up** stairs/curb. (**Good** people go **up** to heaven.)
- The **bad** leg goes first **down** stairs/curb. (**Bad** people go **down** to hell.)
- The "good" leg does all of the work; the "bad" leg goes along for the ride.
- It is harder going **down** stairs and hills; the muscles work harder and there is more pressure on the knee cap (patella). Try walking sideways; the bad leg stepping down first.
- If a railing is available, use on the uninjured side.
- If walking or exercise causes increased pain or swelling, **stop!** If the injured area moves more freely and is less painful, it is OK.

Inflammation

When tissue is hot to touch, **red**, **swollen, and painful**, **it is inflamed**. The body sends blood and lymph to an injured area for healing. However, the extra fluid adds pressure to the tissues, causing increased pain and stiffness.

Ice, applied three to five times a day, is best for inflammation. When the body recognizes the area is getting too cold, it responds by sending more blood to warm the tissues. Therefore, not only does ice decrease swelling, numb pain, and relax muscles, it also increases circulation.

Ice initially causes **vasoconstriction** (closing of vessels and decreasing blood flow). Then, within five minutes, there is **vasodilation** (opening of the blood vessels). Increased blood flow brings more nutrition and oxygen, and flushes toxins and waste products, thus aiding in the healing process.

Gentle movement and massage (stroking toward the heart) decrease swelling, and help scar tissue align more normally and become more flexible. Gentle exercise decreases swelling because muscle contractions pump fluid toward the heart. Elevation, ideally above the level of the heart, and compression decrease swelling as well.

The sooner swelling goes away the better; within 24 hours the fluid begins to turn into scar tissue. Injured tissues become stiff quickly, especially with swelling. Avoid re-injury to prevent additional swelling/scar tissue.

-itis (Inflammation)

-*itis* means inflammation. So by definition:

- **Arthritis.** Inflammation of a joint (arthro)
- **Bursitis.** Inflammation of a bursa (sac of fluid between bones and muscles)
- **Tendonitis.** Inflammation of a tendon, which attaches a muscle to the bone

Ice is best with inflammation (hot, red, swollen, painful tissue); use frequently, three to five times a day (see pages 62-67). Ice vasoconstricts, then vasodilates blood vessels, which increases blood flow. This promotes healing by flushing waste and bringing good nutrition and oxygen.

Arthritis

Arthritis means inflammation of a joint (arthro). However, when people speak of arthritis, they are generally describing **degenerative joint disease (DJD)**, which is wear and tear of the bones and joints. This occurs with age or injury. X-rays may show arthritic (bony) changes, like bone spurs or uneven joint surfaces, but these changes may not cause pain.

Degenerative joint disease, also known as **osteoarthritis**, is very common and often affects the neck, back, knees, hips, thumbs, and the first two joints in the fingers and toes. Some arthritic conditions can be inherited.

There are other types of arthritis, including rheumatoid arthritis, which often affects knees, elbows, and the large knuckles of the hands and feet. Rheumatologists are specialized medical doctors who assess different types of inflammatory diseases.

Even with arthritis, the body can be pain free and fully functional by maintaining good posture, joint motion, muscle flexibility, and strength. If necessary, changes in life style can decrease stress and strain to the arthritic joints. For example, walking is less strenuous than running; biking and water exercise further decrease impact to the back and legs.

Bursitis

Bursitis is inflammation of a bursa (a sac of fluid, which helps muscles move smoothly over other muscles or bones). Bursitis can be very painful and have a rapid onset.

Bursae are located in various places in the body. Typically bursitis occurs at the shoulder or hip. Pain at the outside of the hip, especially when lying on that side, could be caused by bursitis. Ice is most helpful in decreasing pain and swelling (see pages 62-67). A doctor may inject the bursa.

Bursitis in the shoulder will cause a very sharp pinching pain at the top of the shoulder, especially when trying to lift the arm. However, the shoulder could have sharp impinging pains for other reasons, including tight muscles, which do not allow the shoulder joint to move properly. A complete shoulder evaluation will provide an accurate assessment.

Tendonitis

Tendonitis is inflammation of a tendon (connecting muscle to bone). For example, "tennis elbow" is tendonitis of the muscles on the lateral (outside) of the elbow.

Ice is nice! Ice is best for tendonitis because it numbs the pain, takes away swelling, and relaxes muscles. Use ice at least three to five times a day. Ice massage is a quick method of cooling tissues (see pages 64-66). After using ice, gently stretch.

General rules for stretching:
- Stretch slowly and gently, usually about ten repetitions, hold about ten seconds, three times a day.
- Stretch if there is increased motion and decreased pain. **Stop** when pain increases and motion decreases.

Gradually increase pain-free activities; avoid repetitive motions. It is important to not cause pain or swelling so tissues can heal.

General rules for strengthening:
- Gradually build up to three sets of ten repetitions, once a day.
- Exercise only to fatigue; **stop** before onset of pain.

Noises (Crepitation)

Crepitation refers to noise. This includes:

- **Popping** like a knuckle-popping sound. This could be caused by suction, a gas bubble popping, or fluid moving in the joint. Popping is not a problem; in fact it may provide symptom relief. Some people pop more than others.

- **Grinding** like sandpaper. This often occurs with age or injury. It can be annoying, but not necessarily painful. Try to avoid because bone or cartilage may be grinding away. For example, do only pain-free/grind-free and therefore small (not deep) knee bends.

- **Snapping** like a rope. This is probably a tendon snapping, usually not painful, but repeated snapping can cause pain and inflammation, so avoid if possible.

- **Clunking** deep sound. This may be a bone catching on cartilage or a ligament, usually in the shoulder or hip. Usually not painful, but best to avoid.

Sprain

A sprain is injury to ligaments (connecting bone to bone), for example, a sprained ankle. Sprains usually occur with quick unexpected movements resulting in stretched or torn ligaments. Ligaments are not very elastic; they have poor blood supply and are slow to heal. When torn, they may not repair themselves and the joint might be unstable. Strong muscles, bracing, or surgery may be required to provide stability.

Ligaments can take up to one year to heal. Morning stiffness generally indicates ligament damage because ligaments get stiff and sore with inactivity. Increased pain as the day progresses suggests muscle fatigue.

When first injured, use ice to decrease inflammation. Heat is better when the injured area is more stiff than painful. The body will know whether ice or heat is preferred with decreased pain and increased motion. See pages 62-67 for ice and heat instructions.

With time, restore motion with gentle exercise, working with a pain-free range of motion. Then, progress to pain-free strengthening and balance activities; resume normal activities gradually, without increased pain or swelling.

Strain

A strain is an injury to a muscle and/or its tendon, which connects the muscle to the bone. With activity, muscles may fatigue or become sore. If overused, there may be pain and damage to tissues. A muscle needs at least 24 hours to recover. For example, body-builders tend to work their upper body one day and their lower body the next.

Ice three to five times each day with an acute injury (heat, red, swelling, pain). As the muscles become less sore, or more stiff than painful, switch to heat (see pages 62-67). A muscle strain usually takes two to three weeks to heal depending on the extent of the damage.

Bodies become stiff quickly; **keep moving** to avoid losing motion. Stretching later to regain motion can be very painful. The body tells what is best:

- Movement should increase the range of motion (ROM) and decrease pain.
- If movement increases pain and decreases motion, **stop!**

Pain

Pain is a protective mechanism. For example, when stepping on a thorn, the leg will instinctively lift in response to pain.

Pain stops motion so an injured area can heal. Muscle spasms are a built-in response to injury. When a caveman broke a leg, muscle spasms kept the bone from moving so it could heal. Today, bodies still respond the same way.

The body's response to an injury is to send blood and other fluids to the area to start the healing process. Swelling is painful because it increases pressure on tissues. Pain/swelling is supposed to be short-lived and go away as the body heals. At times, assistance is needed in managing both pain and swelling.

Pain versus the Problem

Where pain is felt is not necessarily where the problem is.

Examples:

- Pain felt down the arm could be from a shoulder problem. However, neck or rib problems could be causing similar symptoms.

- A pinch felt at the top of the shoulder may be caused by tight muscles elsewhere in the shoulder area.

- One "stuck" sacro-iliac joint may cause pain in the other SIJ because it is moving too much.

- Back or buttock pain could be caused by a problem on the opposite side, the front of the body, the pelvis, or the hips.

- Symptoms radiating into the leg could be coming from the back or pelvis, possibly from a muscle, joint, or disc problem.

The Body Can Lie

Pain may be felt in one part of the body but originate elsewhere. The body can also *refer* other symptoms, including sensations of hot or cold, pins and needles, tingling, numbness, or heaviness. Sometimes pressure on nerves sends symptoms elsewhere in the body. Neck problems can cause arm symptoms. Low back problems can cause leg symptoms. A body part may *feel* cold, but if it is not cold to touch, it is a referred symptom. If the area is actually cold to touch, there may be a blood flow problem.

The more severe the problem, the larger the area of symptoms. The larger the joint, the more vague the pain. The shoulder is a good example: the farther down the arm the symptoms, the worse the problem; the source of the problem is usually not where the pain is felt.

When pressed, a **trigger point** (tight, tender area in a muscle) can send a variety of symptoms to other parts of the body. Numerous books show where trigger points are located and their referred symptoms.

Pain Control

One way to control pain is to send another message that arrives before the pain. While some nerves send pain messages, other nerves send temperature, motion, or pressure messages to the brain.

Ice, heat, massage, motion, electrical stimulation, and positioning are some ways to counteract pain. Because the same nerves carry hot and cold sensations, a cool compress on a hot injured area will confuse the brain and decrease pain. Pain-relieving lotions and gels work because the brain perceives the sensation of warmth or coolness, which blocks at least some of the pain messages.

Tricking the Body

Pain is perceived in the brain. When another message gets to the brain faster than the pain message, the pain will not be felt so much. Different techniques to help relieve pain work on different parts of the body. Examples:

- **Move** the arm after smashing a thumb. Shoulders and knees hurt less with movement.

- **Rub** the shin after it has been hit or scraped.

- **Cold or heat**, including gels/lotions/oils that give a sensation of hot or cold, will decrease the intensity of the pain. See pages 61-67.

- **Electricity**, including **TNS**, or **TENS** (transcutaneous electrical nerve stimulation), can be effective to block pain. A TENS is a battery-operated portable device with electrodes attached to the body. The intensity and other variables are adjusted to best block pain. Some people like using electricity for pain relief, others do not. If not comfortable, do not use. A TENS unit may feel good, but it does not heal the body. Consult a health care professional for a TENS prescription and instruction in its use.

- **Vibration** can be pain relieving for some.

Goop

Most pain-relieving gels, lotions, and oils provide relief by tricking the brain. The hot or cool sensations travel to the brain faster than the pain. Since the same nerves carry hot and cold messages to the brain, try a cool lotion to counteract a burning sensation.

Use whatever product feels best, but recognize, while it may help control pain, it does not physically heal the body. Ice and heat not only feel good and relieve pain but help the body heal by improving circulation.

Hot or Cold?

Ice is best:

- When applied immediately after an injury. If swelling occurs instantly at the time of injury, blood vessels have been broken, which will show up as bruising. Apply ice and compression to decrease the internal bleeding.

- When pain is acute, sharp, and intense. Intensity of five to ten on a scale of ten.

- When muscles are in spasm.

- When an area is inflamed (painful, red, hot to touch, and swollen).

Ice and heat can be alternated to further enhance blood flow.

Heat is best:

- To relieve achiness and stiffness; to warm the tissues and increase motion.

- If pain is low grade, intensity of five or less.

- When there is no acute inflammation indicated by heat or redness.

- For chronic (on-going) problems that are more stiff than painful.

YOUR BODY BOOK

The body has built-in healing and protective mechanisms. When injured, the body responds immediately by sending extra blood and lymph, which carry oxygen and nutrition for healing. Too much fluid can lead to local congestion. If wastes are not carried away quickly, the area becomes inflamed (hot, red, swollen, and painful).

Ice cools the area, causes vasoconstriction, decreases blood flow, and numbs the pain. However, within five minutes of icing, the blood flow increases and warms the tissues because the body recognizes the tissues are too cold.

Heat causes vasodilation resulting in increased blood flow. Heat also warms the tissues allowing for increased flexibility. **Therefore, both ice and heat increase blood flow, which helps the body heal.**

Ice is Nice

Ice is wonderful, especially with acute and/or recent injuries, muscle spasms, and sharp pinching pain.

- As an anti-inflammatory, ice takes away swelling.

- It numbs the tissue, relieves pain, itching or other symptoms.

- It relaxes muscles.

- It vasoconstricts the first five minutes, decreasing blood flow to the tissue.

- It vasodilates after the first five minutes, opening blood vessels for oxygen and nutrition and flushing toxins and acids.

When swelling occurs instantly at time of injury, blood vessels have been damaged and bruising will occur. Apply ice and compression immediately to limit bruising (see **R.I.C.E.**, page 65).

Ice frequently, for five to twenty minutes, three to five times each day. For ice, use: flexible ice packs, bags of frozen vegetables, frozen popcorn kernels, or make alcohol slush mixtures (see page 66). Use a frozen water bottle, or do ice massage (see next page).

Ice will feel **Cold**, then **Burn**, then **Ache**; then the tissues will feel **Numb (CBAN)**.

YOUR BODY BOOK   65

Ice Massage.

- Freeze water in a paper cup; tear off the top of the cup.

- Rub the ice over the painful area three to five minutes until the tissues are numb and no longer painful when pressed.

- The tissues will feel **Cold**, then **Burn**, then **Ache**, and then **Numb** (**CBAN**).

- When tissues turn white, they are cold enough, **stop** icing. As the body warms, the area will become bright pink with lots of blood flowing.

R.I.C.E. (Rest, Ice, Compress, and Elevate).

R.I.C.E. is ideal for treating swollen painful injuries such as sprained ankles, wrists, and elbows.

- For compression, apply an elastic bandage to the injured area, with overlapping and spiral wrapping toward the heart. Soak the wrap in cool water prior to use for additional cooling. The wrap can also be rolled, placed in a sealable bag, soaked in rubbing alcohol, and kept in the freezer/cooler, for a very cold but flexible wrap.

- Apply ice packs around the injured area.

- Elevate the injured area, ideally above the heart.

- Rest to allow for decreased pain and initial healing.

Ice Packs.

- Can be purchased and should be flexible. Bags of frozen vegetables or popcorn kernels work well. Place a warm wet towel between the skin and the ice pack to increase comfort and improve the cold penetration. Frozen bean bags or rice socks can be used (see next page).

- **Cold**, **Burn**, **Ache**, and then **Numbness (CBAN)** will be felt. When the tissues are numb, remove the ice pack, and allow the area to warm. A too-cold ice pack will cause stinging and may cause frostbite. Remove immediately!

Alcohol Slush Packs.

- Mix two parts water with one part rubbing alcohol in a sealable plastic bag. Place inside a second bag to protect against leaks. Freeze. If too slushy, add more water; if too solid, add more alcohol.

- Place warm wet towel between the ice pack and skin.

- This is antifreeze. **Do not** place directly on the skin; stinging and frostbite may occur.

Ice frequently, up to twenty minutes at a time, three to five times a day.

Heat

Heat usually feels good and is best used with chronic (long-term) injuries and when more stiff than painful. Heat includes showers/baths, hot tubs, hot packs, heating pads, or heated rice socks. Heat improves circulation by vasodilation, which promotes increased oxygen and nutrition, and carries away waste including acids and toxins.

Use heat frequently, twenty minutes every hour, as needed. **Do not** sleep with a heating pad turned on because this could cause a burn. Stretching while in a shower or hot tub is even more beneficial to increase motion and decrease pain.

Rice socks are ideal and can be used day and night. Use around the neck for support and comfort or as a low back support. When traveling, rice socks are useful because microwaves are readily available.

Rice Socks. Pour about two pounds of uncooked rice into a long sock. Tie/sew to close. Place in microwave for about two minutes or until comfortably warm. Rice socks can be frozen as well.

Posture/Positioning

Often, pain is caused by poor posture or positioning. Improving posture and changing positions can eliminate pain.

Bad posture/position:

- **Prolonged sitting**, greater than 20 minutes, puts additional stress on the back and can cause disc bulging. When sitting, muscles tighten; this limits the ability to stand and causes back pain.

- **Forward head** posture, or "*goose necking*," compresses the back of the neck. This can cause pain, fatigue, and headaches. It can also compress the nerves that run into the arm causing symptoms like pain, pins and needles, tingling, numbness, and weakness.

- **Pillows** that are too thick or thin do not support the neck well. Neck joints can become pinched, or overly stretched; muscles can spasm, resulting in pain.

- **Clenched** teeth can cause pain and headaches.

Good posture/positions:

- **Sit tall**. A low back support should be comfortable and decrease back pain; a rice sock (see page 67) can be used. In addition, perform a few gentle back bends after sitting (see page 115).

- **Stand tall**. Place one foot up on a stool to prevent slouching when working at a counter.

- Keep **chin tucked**. The back of the head should touch the headrest when driving. Be sure glasses are adjusted correctly for reading books and computer screens. Use a headset on the phone to prevent side-bent positioning.

- Pull **shoulders back and down**.

- **Tilt the pelvis** to flatten the back and stomach.

- **Bend knees slightly**, not locked, when standing.

- Keep **teeth slightly separated** except when chewing food. TMJ (jaw) rotation exercises can relieve pain (see page 105).

- **Move**, fidget, change positions frequently; take stretch breaks.

Positioning for Pain Relief

Stop pain and muscle spasms with positioning. Strain-Counterstrain, or positional release, can stop pain in 90 seconds:

- Locate a tender point; pick the most tender if there are several.

- Find a position of comfort, so the tender point is no longer sore when pressed.

- Stay relaxed in that position for **90 seconds or more**; then slowly return to normal position.

- Repeat as necessary.

For example, with a tender point on the left side of the neck, gently tilt the head to the left, turn the head a little left or right, depending on which direction relaxes the muscle.

Necks like to be supported, particularly at night; custom-fit a rice sock or experiment with pillows. Sometimes a head feels too heavy because the small neck muscles become tired of balancing ten or more pounds; lie down, or lean against a headrest to rest the neck.

Backs tend to be most comfortable when lying on the back, with legs supported on pillows. Let the knees slightly separate (frog-leg position) and relax the back and buttock muscles. Because the body weighs less in water, spend time in pools or baths for pain relief.

YOUR BODY BOOK

Painful shoulders do not like to be slept on. Sleep on the opposite side and use a pillow under the sore arm for support. If sleeping on the back, place pillows under the arm. Try resting in a recliner with pillows supporting the arm. Shoulders are most comfortable when arms are placed about 60 degrees away from the body, which is what a pillow provides. A small towel roll or pillow in the axilla (armpit) can help too.

Shoulders like to move, so gentle motion and stretching will help them feel better. Shoulders are more painful at night because of immobility and increased pressure. Any pain may be worse at night because it is dark, quiet, and the brain has nothing else to think about besides the pain.

Knees are most comfortable at a 30 degree bend. Place a pillow under the knees when lying on the back. A pillow between the knees when lying on the side decreases strain to the back, pelvis, hips, and knees.

Pillows

Pillows are useful to relieve pain. Customize the pillow for support. Rice socks, bean bags, or rolled towels can support the neck or back. A heated or cooled support increases pain relief.

Pillows under the arm will decrease stress to the neck and shoulders. A pillow under the knee opens the joint space and decreases pressure. Pillows between the legs, when lying on the side, decreases strain to the back, pelvis, hips, and knees. A long **body pillow** supports both the arm and the leg, or can be placed behind the body to lean against.

Pillows, a triangular wedge, or bolster (block of foam about 14 inches tall) placed under the legs takes pressure off the spine when lying on the back.

Massage/Manual Therapy

Massage and manual therapy range from light to very deep "hurt so good" hands-on techniques.

- **Lymphatic drainage** or **retrograde massage** helps to decrease swelling. Very light pressure moves lymph fluid just under the skin.

- **Cranial Sacral Therapy** is a very gentle manual therapy technique. Cranial (head) Sacral (tail bone) Therapy is a head-to-tail treatment. It tunes into the cerebral spinal fluid flowing around the brain and spinal cord. As the flow improves, nerves receive nutrition and function better; this helps the body heal.

- **Swedish Massage** begins with light stroking, working deeper as the body allows.

- **Myofascial Release** is slow deep massage to the muscle (myo) and fascia (thick connective tissue).

- **Acupressure** is sustained pressure, usually about 30 seconds, to specific points on the body.

- **Trigger Point Release** can include pressing a tight, tender area in the muscle, with increasing pressure as tolerated for up to 60 seconds, then slowly release (see page 58).

- **Skin lifting/rolling** can be very uncomfortable if the skin has become adhered to other tissues. With an injury, swelling occurs. Within 24 hours, the swelling starts to turn into scar tissue; sometimes tissues become stuck together. Tissues are supposed to be pain free, flexible, and have the same thickness as similar parts of the body. Lift the skin off the body and move it in different directions. If the skin feels thick, tight, or stuck, work to restore its flexibility with massage and progress to literally lifting the skin off the tissues below. This should be done once a day, for about a minute or as tolerated.

- **Friction Massage, cross-fiber massage** is deep and specific rubbing across a tissue. Locate the most tender point on the tendon or ligament; rub for about a minute, once a day. If the tissue becomes less sensitive while massaging, this is good; **stop** immediately when the area becomes more sore. The goal is to stimulate blood flow, and to help the tissues correctly line up with parallel fibers.

III. Health Tips

Improved physical health
can bring mental, emotional,
and spiritual benefits.

Water

Every part of the body — including the brain — needs ample water. Good blood flow brings in oxygen and nutrition and carries out waste products including toxins and acids. The digestive system needs fluid to process and expel waste. Fluid is required for good lubrication and nutrition in joints. Water is even in bones and cartilage.

Discs, the cushions between the back vertebrae, are sponge-like. Discs absorb fluid when lying down; after sleeping, the back may have lengthened by an inch. As the day progresses, the fluid is squeezed out. It is common to tilt the rear view mirror *up* in the morning and readjust it *down* later in the day. With age, discs tend to dry and become thinner, which is a reason why people become shorter. Drinking water may help keep the discs healthier.

Water can help the body heal, especially when trying to reduce inflammation (swelling). Drinking water is recommended before and after massage and exercise to promote elimination of waste products, including acids and toxins. This can prevent nausea or feeling ill; it may also help decrease soreness or stiffness, which can occur following massage and exercise.

Nutrition

The body is a finely-tuned machine and needs good fuel to run efficiently. Better nutrition results in a healthier body, which feels better too. Basic nutrition includes:

- Drink water. The body needs adequate blood to carry oxygen and nutrition throughout the body and to the brain. Fluid is needed to eliminate waste.

- The more natural the food the better.

- Eat fruits, vegetables, beans, whole grains, nuts, and seeds; these contain fiber, vitamins, and minerals. The more rainbow-colored the food, the better.

- Eat foods with high fiber, low fat, and low animal protein. Only a few ounces of protein a day are needed, which is about the size of a deck of cards, or what fits in the palm of your hand.

- Limit processed foods, animal fat, and red meat, with minimal intake of dairy and eggs. Toxins are stored in animal fat, including *your* fat. Decreasing intake of animal products and decreasing personal body fat should improve health and may prevent disease.

YOUR BODY BOOK

- Avoid sugar; it is an inflammatory agent.

- Reduce or eliminate caffeine, soda, and alcohol.

- Food *allergies* can cause symptoms such as headaches, rashes, pain, tender points, and fatigue. Some people may be *sensitive* to dairy products, gluten, sugar, and/or other foods.

- Vitamin and mineral supplements may be needed, especially calcium, vitamin D3, and vitamin B12. Talk to health care providers about supplements.

Sleep

If you can't sleep, you can't heal. If you can't sleep, you may become depressed. If you can't sleep, you might gain weight. If you can't sleep, you probably won't feel good, let alone awake with energy.

Adults usually need at least 7-8 hours of sleep a day with a minimum of four hours of **deep sleep**. A comfortable mattress is a must, and a pillow that provides good neck support. Lying on the side, or on the back with pillows beneath the knees, is good; sleeping on the stomach is not. If stress causes loss of sleep, ways to self-manage include: keep a journal, make lists, meditate, and use relaxation techniques. Night sweats and hormonal changes can contribute to sleep loss. If not sleeping well, talk to health care providers for assistance.

Pain is usually worse at night. It is dark, quiet, and the brain has nothing better to do than tune into the pain. Ligaments become stiff with immobility and can become painful. Body fluid shifts: when lying down, it flows horizontally; when standing, it flows down. Shoulder pain increases at night because of increased fluid pressure and stiffness. Backs become more stiff and painful as the discs fill with fluid.

If pain prevents sleep, try ice, heat, lotion/gels, TENS (transcutaneous electrical nerve stimulation), pillows, and positioning (see pages 60-72). Gentle movement exercises/stretching, especially before getting out of bed, decreases pain/stiffness, increases motion, and prepares the body for the day's activities. Pelvic tilts and knee-to-chest stretching exercises are helpful to decrease low back pain/stiffness; see page 112.

Medication

Consult your physician about medications.
When injured, use ice first. Ice works as an anti-inflammatory; it decreases swelling, relaxes muscles, and relieves pain. In addition, an anti-inflammatory medication may be recommended (such as aspirin, naproxen, or ibuprofen). Do not mix these medications. It is important to take as prescribed, if no adverse side effects. Take consistently, keeping a steady dose in the body, to be most effective.

If anti-inflammatory medication does not provide enough pain relief, a muscle relaxer or pain medication may be prescribed. Take them as needed; they may improve sleep as well. Medication should be decreased and stopped as soon as possible so the body does not become dependent or suffer from adverse side effects.

Discuss all your medications and supplements with your health care provider.

Posture

Good posture keeps the body aligned and prevents muscles from becoming too tight and sore, or too stretched and painful.

Ideal posture includes:

- Chin tucked in to keep the head balanced on the neck. Back of the head should touch the car headrest.

- Shoulders back, down, and level, arms at the side of the body, not toward the front.

- Pelvis tilted to decrease excessive curvature of the low back and stomach protrusion.

- Knees slightly bent. Locked knees are not good because ligaments may become overly stretched.

- Legs positioned symmetrically (the same) and equal length; ideally with toes pointed straight ahead.

See pages 68-69 for additional information about posture.

Changing Positions (Transfers)

- **Log Roll**. To get into bed: sit; lie down onto side, bring legs onto the bed. With knees bent, roll onto back. To get out of bed: roll onto side with knees bent; push up with arms as feet go down to the floor. Once sitting, make sure you are not light-headed or dizzy before coming to stand.

- **Sit-to-Stand**. Scoot forward on the chair. Then, use arms to push up. Before sitting, reach back for the chair/bed/toilet. Reaching back ensures the seat is close enough to be safe and the arms can assist in sitting down slowly and smoothly.

- If using a walker, cane or crutches, stand first, and then grasp the walking aid. Before sitting, let go of walking aide and reach back for the seat.

- To get into a car, first sit, and then swing in legs. To get out, swing both legs before standing. If it hurts to lift a leg, use arms to help.

Body Mechanics

Good body positions decrease strain to the body and prevent injuries. Use the best muscles for the job; let big/strong muscles work to avoid straining small muscles.

- Avoid bending forward. Half of the body weight pulls on the back when bending. This strains the small back muscles and increases pressure on the discs. Instead, use the large leg muscles to squat and lift, while keeping the back straight. When lifting, keep objects close to the trunk.

- Keep the chin tucked (see page 106). The head weighs about ten pounds; a forward head stresses the neck and back.

- Avoid repetitive twisting. Turn by moving the legs rather than twisting from the back or hips. If moving repetitively in one direction, change directions. For example, if shoveling to the right, at times shovel to the left.

- When shoveling, raking, sweeping, and vacuuming, use the legs (stepping forward, backward, or sideways) rather than moving the arms.

- Sit with good back support. Try a small pillow or rolled towel in the small of the back. Sitting slumped increases pressure on discs. Sit for less than 20 minutes at a time to prevent excessive disc pressure.

YOUR BODY BOOK

Balance

To improve balance, practice standing on one foot. Stand next to a counter or railing as needed for safety. Standing on a soft surface such as a couch cushion and/ or balancing with eyes closed is more challenging. It is best to practice barefoot. The goal is to balance at least ten seconds on each leg.

For improved leg strength, do **small** squats (about a 30 degree knee bend), pain free, without popping/ grinding of the knee cap (patella). Standing on one leg *and* doing small squats improves both strength and balance. Build up to 30 or more repetitions.

For additional strength, balance, and coordination, walk: forward, backward, sideways, on toes, on heels, heel-to-toe with one foot directly in front of the other. Use a counter or railing as needed for safety.

Balance activities are usually done once a day, about five minutes or more until tired.

Flexibility

Flexibility allows motion, which is how joints are lubricated and receive nutrition. Good motion should be maintained in every part of the body. Loss of flexibility can affect posture, balance, strength, and function thus limiting your normal lifestyle.

Stretch before and after physical activity and exercise to decrease stiffness, soreness, and injury to muscles. Some people need to stretch often to maintain or become more flexible. A *daily* stretching exercise program is ideal for maintaining good body motion (see page 102).

Flexibility, in part, is genetic. Some people are more flexible than others. Some can touch their toes; others can place their hands flat on the floor, while others may do well to reach below their knees. Women tend to be more flexible than men, and become more flexible during pregnancy and mid-menstrual cycle.

Being too flexible can be a problem. If ligaments are loose, joints may move too much and not be stable. It is easier to stretch tight tissue than tighten loose tissues. Once overstretched, ligaments may not regain their normal length and strength.

Shorter With Age

Discs are cushions between back bones (vertebrae). In the neck and mid back, discs are very thin; low back discs can be about ¼ inch thick. With sleep, discs fill with fluid and the body is taller by about an inch. As the day progresses, the fluid is squeezed out and the body gradually shortens. At the beginning of the day, it is common to tilt the rear view mirror *up*, and at the end of the day to tilt it *down*.

Disc material is more sponge-like when young. With age, discs are less able to absorb fluid. With wear-and-tear, discs become damaged and thinner; the body becomes shorter. Sometimes vertebrae can become compressed. Compression fractures usually occur in the mid back (the thoracic spine) and can be painful for months. Poor posture, weakness, and osteoporosis (loss of bone density) also contribute to becoming shorter with age.

To avoid shrinking:

- Drink water.
- Eat bone-healthy foods (with calcium/vitamin D3) and take supplements/medications if recommended by your doctor.
- Maintain good posture. Stand tall!
- Stretch to keep flexible, especially the chest muscles (see page 108), at least once a day.
- Strengthen, especially the back muscles, at least twice a week.
- Walk and/or do other weight-bearing activities, to keep bones strong.
- Do balance exercises to avoid falls and injuries.

For Women Only: Hormones

Hormonal cycles affect the body. When a woman ovulates, at about day 14 of her cycle, her hormones change. The body becomes more flexible because ligaments become more elastic. This lasts until menstruation begins. A woman needs to be elastic when pregnant to allow for the growing baby, but it is not helpful when the body is trying to heal from an injury.

Women can be more uncomfortable during this phase of their cycle, usually with complaints of achiness. Because ligaments hold joints together; joints can become less stable and more easily out of alignment during this time. Sacro-iliac joints (SIJ) are especially vulnerable because they are held together only with ligaments; there are no muscles to maintain alignment.

Water retention places more pressure on nerves and increases discomfort. Other premenstrual symptoms — decreased pain tolerance, poor balance, and emotional changes — can frustrate recovery from an injury. Hormonal imbalances can also contribute to sleep loss.

Weather

"I can feel it in my bones; it's going to rain."

When the weather is going to change, there is a change in the atmospheric pressure. Barometers show the increase or decrease in air pressure. Air pressure also changes with elevation when driving through mountains or flying.

The body is a finely-tuned instrument and is very sensitive to pressure changes. As air pressure changes, body pressure adjusts; this can take about 24 hours.

Some people are more aware of, and sensitive to, weather and pressure changes. If a joint or tissue is swollen, pressure changes can be even more apparent. Joints will often become more achy and stiff. Gentle exercise and heat can sometimes help decrease discomfort.

On the Road Again

Some suggestions when traveling:

- Keep moving to reduce stiffness, soreness, and potential blood clots. Change positions (at least every 30 minutes), fidget, and do isometric exercises — contract and relax muscles — to increase blood flow and prevent swelling.

- Do neck stretches, shoulder shrugs and circles to decrease muscle tension and stress.

- Stop at rest areas and walk around.

- Standing back bends decrease back strain and stretch the hip muscles that shorten with prolonged sitting (see page 115).

- Keep knees moving; they stiffen quickly with immobility. Standing small squats are quick and easy and should be pain free (see page 120).

- Use a rice sock (two pounds of uncooked rice in a long sock, tie/sew to close) to provide support, decrease pain and stiffness. It can be chilled in refrigerator, freezer, or cooler, or heated in a microwave for about two minutes.

- Take sealable plastic bags for crushed ice.

- Be aware of air pressure changes affecting the body. Changing elevation and/or weather changes may cause symptoms.

It's an Emergency!

It *is* an **emergency** if a person experiences:

- **A sudden loss of bowel or bladder control.**

- **Falling because a leg gives way.**

- **Symptoms radiating down both legs or both arms.** The spinal cord itself may be compressed — rather than just nerves on either side of the spine.

- **Paralysis or significant weakness.** For example: if unable to walk on toes or heels, or a noticeably weak grip. Pressure on sensory nerves going to the brain causes pain and other symptoms; this can be very distressing. However, pressure on motor nerves, running from the brain to the body, is more serious because it causes weakness. Depending on which nerves are compressed, there can be a major loss of function including inability to walk or control of bowel or bladder.

Seek medical attention immediately!

Perspective (Time to Heal)

The good news is the body does its best to mend, especially with orthopedic injuries, which affect bones, joints, and muscles.

Injuries take time to heal; broken (fractured) **bones** usually take six weeks. **Muscles** begin to heal within 24 hours but can take two or more weeks to heal completely. **Tendons,** which connect muscles to bones, can take six weeks to begin to heal. **Ligaments**, connecting bone to bone, can take a year to heal. Ligaments are like ropes with very little elasticity and poor circulation. Tissues with poor blood supply take longer to heal.

Nerves can take a year or more to heal — if they do heal. Nerves grow about as fast as hair. If a nerve is compressed, it can be damaged temporarily, like when a limb "falls asleep" and tingles on awakening, or it can be damaged permanently.

The body responds to injury by sending blood and lymph to the area, which results in swelling. Within 24 hours, the swelling begins to turn into scar tissue. In scar tissue is collagen, a toothpick-shaped cell, which lives almost a year. **Scar tissue** continues to change as old scar cells die and are replaced with new cells. Especially during the first year of healing, scar tissue can be modified to be less dense and more flexible; massage and exercise are helpful.

Getting Better

Help the body heal. Priorities include:

- **Managing pain**. This includes use of: ice, heat, gels/lotions, rest, pillows, positioning, motion, and possible medication (for swelling, relaxing muscles, pain, depression, and sleep).

- **Sleeping; if you can't sleep, you can't heal and you may become depressed**.

- **Improving blood flow**. Blood carries oxygen and nutrition. Blood flow removes acids and toxins, which cause pain and burning. Improving circulation with ice, heat, and motion promotes healing.

- **Assessing and correcting alignment** of the body.

- Restoring **range of motion (ROM)**. The body needs to move correctly before strengthening.

- **Pain-free strengthening** and gradually return to normal **Activities of Daily Living (ADLs)**.

- Strengthening activities promote core strength, aerobic conditioning, endurance, power, and speed.

A general rule of thumb: For every "down" day, it takes two to three days to recover.

Stress

Mental and/or emotional stress can lead to, or aggravate, physical problems. Stress can cause muscles to tighten, decrease blood flow, fluid congestion, and buildup of toxins and acids. Stress can decrease sleep, which can slow healing and increase pain.

Pain is fatiguing; so is managing pain. Adding stress is even more exhausting. An injury can affect every part of a person's life. Worrying, especially about things out of your control, can be overwhelming.

Focus on what *you can do* to help your body to heal. Think positively. Break overwhelming tasks and issues into small, do-able steps.

Ways to decrease stress: exercise, take a walk, breathe deeply, meditate, perform relaxation techniques, and write thoughts and concerns in a journal. Accept help from others; seek professional assistance, which could include counseling and/or medications.

Fear

The more you know . . .
the less you have to fear.

- You are fixable! Your body will do its best to heal.

- It takes time to heal; you can help.

- You can better control pain if you are aware of tools you can use — ice, heat, positioning, and appropriate medications.

- Stress, worry, and fear take energy from the healing process; they can also cause loss of sleep. You have tools to help these issues too.

- Gather information so you can better work with health care professionals to successfully manage your health.

Health History/Journal

Keep a health history, especially surgery dates and what was done. Ask for, and keep copies of, medical reports including X-rays, laboratory results, and other tests in a file. Keep a list of current medications, herbs, vitamins, and supplements of any kind; give copies to your health care provider.

Keep a journal to remember and monitor changes. This will help you and health care professionals record changes in **frequency, intensity, duration,** and **area (FIDA)** of symptoms. Pain is usually reported on a scale of 0 to 10, 10 being excruciating pain.

Only you have the whole picture. Actively manage your health. Health care professionals only know what they know and look for what they are looking for. Keep a journal and share your history with your medical team; this will help them to help you. Let them know about: nutrition, medications, supplements, sleep, smoking, exercise, stress, and previous history.

IV. Exercise

Every body needs exercise.

Everybody needs to exercise.

Exercise increases blood flow
to the body and the brain.

With exercise
you will be stronger,
more flexible, and healthier.

Exercise

Every body needs exercise. (Work is not exercise.) Exercise increases freedom of movement and blood flow to all parts of the body, including the brain. It improves strength and sleep, decreases stress, assists in weight control, provides an overall feeling of well-being, and can be fun! There are many types of exercises and reasons to exercise. Listed below are a few:

- **Stress reduction**. Can be as simple as taking deep breaths throughout the day.

- **Aerobic**. Any non-stop motion, like walking, biking, swimming, or dancing, for at least 30 minutes, two to three times a week. This is good for the heart, lungs, and pumps blood throughout the body; this helps us think and feel better.

- **Stretching**. Keeps flexibility and joints healthy with lubrication and nutrition. Stretch at least once a day.

- **Strengthening**. Maintains bones and keeps muscles strong, prevents injuries, and helps with normal activities of daily living (ADLs). Strengthen at least two to three times a week, with a recovery day in between. Body builders exercise their upper body one day, and their lower body the next.

It is never too late to start exercising. Ask your body to do a little more every day. The body will accommodate, move more freely, be stronger, and feel better.

Exercise Myths

- **No pain, no gain**
- **More is better**
- **All or none**

No pain, **no gain** refers only to the temporary burning pain that can occur when exercising. This is because lactic acid builds up in the tissues. When a muscle tightens, the blood flow is shut off; especially with an isometric contraction (no motion occurs). As soon as the muscle relaxes, blood flow returns, the acid is carried away, and the burning is gone!

More is better may be true when strengthening, but must be pain free. When muscles start to feel tired/fatigued, **stop** and wait 24 hours before using them again strenuously. If muscles are pushed past fatigue into pain, they will not become stronger, and will be at more risk of injury.

There is no point to **all or none**; it is better to push a little harder every day and gradually increase flexibility, strength, and endurance. Break large goals into small steps.

The Body's Rules

- Increased motion and/or decreased pain is **good**.
- Pulling/stretching sensation is **OK**.
- If stretching increases motion and decreases pain, it is **OK**.
- Decreased motion and/or increased pain is **bad**.
- Pinching pain is **not OK**.
- Increased intensity or area of pain/symptoms is **not OK**.

Rules for Stretching and Strengthening

Stretching Rules

- If increased motion and decreased pain, keep going.
- If decreased motion or increased pain, **stop!**
- If there is tightness before pain, stretch.
- If there is pain before tightness, go easy.
- Avoid sharp pinching pain.
- Stretch slowly, generally,
    - Three to ten repetitions.
    - One to three times a day.

Strengthening Rules

- Ten or more repetitions.
- Once a day.
- Pain free, or no increase in pain.
- Move smoothly; the slower the better, especially upon release.
- Exercise to fatigue; **stop** before onset of pain.

Use It or Lose It

If you do not use your body, you will lose:

- Motion
- Strength
- Balance
- Function

You need at least 80 % normal motion and strength to do regular activities. Unfortunately, you can sometimes lose 50 % before you even know you are in trouble. For example, a 30-pound grip strength is usually needed to open a jar; women usually have a 60-pound grip, men 80-pounds or more. At the very least, you need to be able to get in/out of bed and on/off toilets and chairs, dress, put on socks and shoes, reach into cupboards, walk, climb stairs, and get up off the floor.

With good flexibility, strength, and balance, the body will be healthier, more responsive to the demands placed on it, and less likely to fall into disrepair. This results in greater freedom to live as you wish.

The exercises listed on the following pages provide the basic stretching and strengthening needed for functional living. Some can be done prior to getting up, others in the shower — with the advantage of the warm water — or standing. They can be incorporated into your life quickly, quietly, and effectively.

Head-to-Toe Exercises

TMJ (Jaw) Rotation

Neck Stretching

Shoulder Stretching and Strengthening

Back Flexion and Extension

Prone Knee Flexion / Hip Rotation

Back Strengthening

Hamstrings Stretching

Calf Stretching

Closed-Chain Strengthening

 Small Squat

 Push-Up

TMJ (Jaw) Rotation Exercise

Six repetitions, six times a day.

Easily done in the shower, while driving, and before eating.

With the tongue touching the roof of the mouth, open and close the mouth. This is a **gentle** exercise; only open as is comfortable. The motion should be **pain free and smooth**. The joint motion should be symmetrical (the same on both sides), and without crepitation (noise including pops, clicks, and grinding). This lubricates the joints, improves motion, reduces pain, and muscle tension.

Neck Stretching Exercises

Three repetitions, move slowly, hold three seconds or more, three times a day. Do in the shower, in the car, with a towel or rice sock for support if desired. Keep shoulders down and back.

- **Chin Tuck.** Lower chin about an inch, creating a double chin, stretching the upper neck muscles at the base of the head.

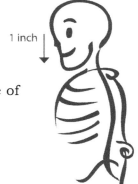

- **Neck Flexion. Chin-to-Chest** stretches muscles on the back of the neck. Then turn the head to the left and right; this stretches muscles at the base of the skull allowing the head to turn on the first two neck vertebrae. Half of the neck's ability to turn occurs in the upper cervical region.

Neck Stretching Exercises (continued)

- **Neck Rotation.** **Turn** head to the left and right. It is important, especially when driving, to be able to turn the head at least 60 degrees, which is 2/3 of the way to the shoulder.

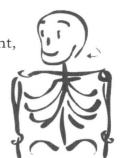

- **Neck Side Bend.** **Tilt** head to the left and right, moving the ear toward the shoulder, without allowing the head to turn.

- **Do not** tilt the head back if it causes dizziness or light-headedness; this could decrease the blood flow to the brain, which is not good. If tilting the head back, try supporting the back of the neck with your fingers, a towel, or rice sock.

Shoulder Exercises

Shoulder Stretching — External Rotation

Ten repetitions, hold at least ten seconds, at least three times a day. Stretching can be uncomfortable, but if the motion improves, keep going. When the shoulder becomes more sore, or starts to lose motion, stop! Can be done lying, sitting, standing, in the shower, walking, or stretching in a doorway.

- **"ER-at-side."** Elbows at the side of the body, elbows bent 90 degrees, move hands away from the stomach. This exercise stretches the subscapularis muscle, which is under the shoulder blade.

- **"Stick-em-up."** With arms elevated to 90 degrees away from the side of the body, elbows bent 90 degrees, move arms back. This stretches a large chest muscle, (pectoralis major) and a smaller muscle, (pectoralis minor).

Shoulder Stretching — Internal Rotation

Ten repetitions, at least three times a day. Stretching can be uncomfortable, but if the motion improves, keep going. When the shoulder becomes more sore, or starts to lose motion, stop! Can be done sitting, standing, when walking, and in the shower.

- **"Chicken wings."** With hands at the waist, or behind the back, move elbows forward and backward. Move only the elbows; do not allow the shoulder blades to move.

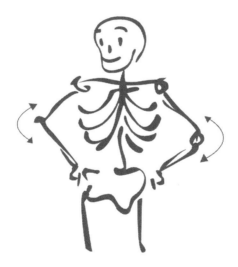

Shoulder Stretching — Flexion

Ten repetitions, hold at least ten seconds, at least three times a day. Stretching can be uncomfortable, but if the motion improves, keep going. When the shoulder becomes more sore, or starts to lose motion, stop! Avoid sharp pinching pain, usually occurring at about 90 degrees elevation.

- **Shoulder flexion.** Reach arms overhead, ideally at least past the eyes. Stretching can be done lying, sitting, standing, in a doorway, or bending forward with hands on a counter/railing. It can be more painful to bring the arm down. Use the "good" arm to assist the "bad" arm. Move the arm slowly and avoid sharp painful positions.

Shoulder Strengthening

Strengthening exercises must be pain free and can be done once a day. Build up to 30 repetitions. Move smoothly; the slower the better, especially upon release. Strengthening exercises include: lifting weights, using a resistance band, and doing push-ups against a wall/counter, or on the floor.

It is important to strengthen the four small rotator cuff muscles. These exercises are especially beneficial:

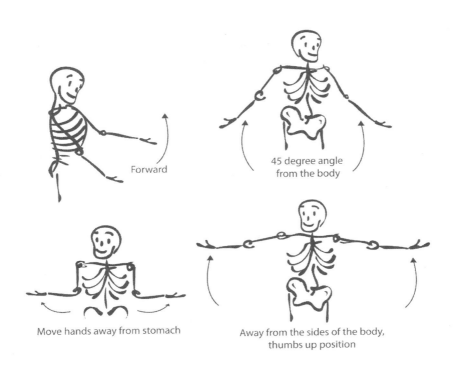

Back Exercises

These exercises should be done gently and help the back feel better. Generally start with stretching; progress to pain-free strengthening.

Back flexion exercises

Three to ten repetitions, hold three to ten seconds, one to three times a day, as needed. Best prior to getting out of bed, can be done on the floor. Lie on back with knees bent.

- **Pelvic tilts**. Press low back to the floor, by tightening the stomach muscles. This stretches, strengthens, and lubricates the low back. Pelvic tilts can also be performed when sitting or standing.

- **Knee-to-chest stretching**. Bring one or both knees toward the chest stretching the low back and buttock muscles. If this feels good, and the back feels better afterwards, it is a good exercise.

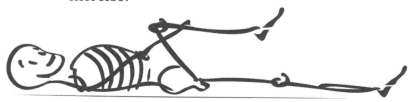

Back flexion strengthening exercises

Build up to 30 times, once a day; must be pain free. Lie on the back (on bed/floor) with knees bent.

- **Curl-ups. Crunches**, not full sit-ups. Lift head and shoulders, tightening stomach muscles but not involving the legs. Arms can be placed across the chest, along the side of the body, behind the head or pointed to the ceiling.

- **Bridges**. Lift hips a few inches. This strengthens the back, buttocks, and leg muscles.

Back extension stretching exercises

These increase the curve of the low back. They can be especially beneficial to decrease pressure on nerves causing back and/or leg symptoms, often present with a disc injury. The goal is centralized (smaller) symptoms in the back and legs. Do as often as needed to decrease symptoms (on bed/floor).

- **Prone-on-elbows.** Up to several minutes, as is comfortable. Lie on stomach, propped up on elbows, with low back relaxed in a swayed-back position.

- **Press-up.** Three to ten repetitions, if increased motion and decreased/centralized symptoms. Lie on stomach, propped on elbows; then straighten elbows, keeping the pelvis on the floor, to increase the arch in the low back.

- **Back bends standing**. Three to ten repetitions, as it feels good, with increased motion and decreased symptoms, as often as needed. Hands, or a towel, for support in the small of the back can help. Look straight ahead; the head should not tilt back. This exercise is especially good after sitting or bending forward.

Prone knee flexion/hip rotation stretching exercises

Three to ten repetitions, once or twice a day, as needed with the goal of good motion (same on each side) and symptom relief. These can be done on the bed/floor or standing, holding onto a counter/railing, without pain, back or pelvic motion.

- **Prone knee flexion stretching.** Lie on stomach; bend one knee to stretch the front thigh muscles. The heel should ideally be about six inches from the buttock.

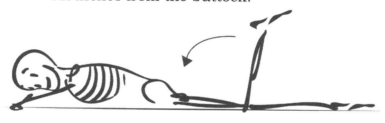

- **Prone hip rotation stretching.** Lie on stomach; bend one knee to 90 degrees, then move that lower leg to the left and right to stretch the hip joint and buttock muscles.

Back Strengthening Exercises

Back exercises include strengthening the abdominal muscles along with *core strengthening* of the deep back/pelvic muscles. Strengthening exercises must be pain free. Perform them smoothly; the slower the better, especially upon release. Generally, strengthening exercises are performed once a day, 10 to 30 repetitions, increasing the number as able. Basic strengthening exercises include:

- **Pelvic Tilts.** See page 112.
- **Curl-ups/crunches.** See page 113.
- **Bridges.** See page 113.
- **Arm and leg lifts,** while lying on stomach or back.

A therapy ball and/or foam roll can be used for strengthening and balance.

Other Stretches

Stretch three to ten repetitions, hold for thirty seconds or more. Do one to three times a day. It is especially important to stretch before and after exercising or playing sports.

- **Hamstrings stretching**. Hamstrings (the muscles on the back of the thigh) flexibility is important for the back, legs, and walking. Hamstrings are large muscles; it takes time and effort to increase their flexibility. One way to stretch hamstrings is to straighten the knee when sitting. For additional stretch, pull toes toward the nose. For even more stretch, bend the head down and/or lean forward, if this does not cause back pain.

- **Gastrocnemius and Soleus stretching.**
  Flexibility of the calf muscles affects the back, knees, ankles, and feet. Calf stretching can be done standing, leaning against a wall or counter, or with the heels hanging off the edge of a step or curb. Stretch the:

  - Gastrocnemius muscle with the knee straight.

  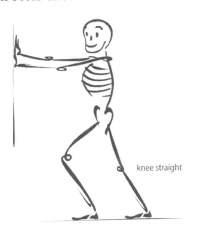

  knee straight

  - Soleus muscle with the knee slightly bent.

  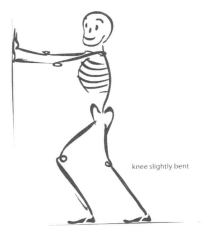

  knee slightly bent

Closed-Chain Strengthening Exercises

Once a day, to fatigue, build up to at least 30 repetitions. To be done pain free, and crepitation free (no noise — snap, crackle, pops).

These provide functional strength; examples include:

- **Small squat.** While standing, do small knee bends. To increase difficulty, stand on one leg. For safety, stand next to, or hold on to, counter/railing. Improved strength increases the ability to get up from chairs, toilets, and beds.

- **Push-up.** Start with push-ups against a wall, progress to a counter, then onto the bed or floor but from the knees. Progress to full push-ups if able, with good trunk control.

YOUR BODY BOOK

Notes
for Your Better Body Health

Notes
for Your Better Body Health

Glossary

Acetabulum — hip socket

Acromion — tip of shoulder blade at top of shoulder

Acupressure — sustained pressure for 30 seconds or more; can be a "hurt so good" sensation but relieves pain upon release

Acute — recent injury or very painful; pain limits motion

ADLs — Activities of Daily Living

Aerobic exercise — non-stop motion for at least 20 minutes

Aligned — in correct position

Anterior — front

Anti-inflammatory — takes away swelling

Arthritis — inflammation of a joint (arthro)

Axilla — arm pit

ASAP — as soon as possible

Bursitis — inflammation of a bursa (sac of fluid located between bone and muscles)

Cerebral spinal fluid (CSF) — fluid flowing around the brain and spinal cord

Cervical vertebrae — seven neck bones

Chondromalacia — softening of cartilage, generally under the knee cap (patella)

Chronic — long-term injury, longer than 6 weeks, often more stiff than painful

Clavicle — collar bone

Coccyx — tail bone at tip of sacrum

Collagen — toothpick-shaped cell included in scar tissue

Cranial Sacral Therapy (CST) — gentle healing manual therapy technique

Crepitation — noise including popping and grinding

DDD — degenerative disc disease

124   YOUR BODY BOOK

Disc — thin cushion between bones, in back and jaw

DJD — degenerative joint disease, also known as osteoarthritis

Extension — for example, bending backward

External Rotation (ER) — rotate away from the body

Facet — joint that connects vertebrae in the spine

Fascia — thick connective tissue

Femur — thigh bone

Fibula — small bone in lower leg, next to tibia

Flexion — for example, bending forward

FIDA — frequency, intensity, duration, area of symptoms

Foramen — opening between each vertebra

Friction massage, cross-fiber massage — specific deep massage across fibers, often used to treat tendonitis

Gastrocnemius — a calf muscle, stretch with knee straight

"Golfer's elbow" — medial epicondylitis, tendonitis on the inside of the elbow

"Goose necking" — forward head posture

Greater trochanter — bump of bone on the femur at the outside of the pelvis

Herniated disc — cracks in the outside cartilage rings of a disc allowed the inside nucleus material to exit

Humerus — upper arm bone

Iliacus — muscle inside the ilium in the anterior pelvis

Ilio-tibial band (ITB) — thick tissue on the outside of thigh

Ilium — large pelvic bones connected to the sacrum at the SIJ (sacro-iliac joints)

Impingement — pinching of tissues, causing pain; can lead to inflammation (swelling) that puts even more pressure on tissues

Inflammation — swelling; with acute inflammation the tissue is hot, red, swollen, and painful

YOUR BODY BOOK

Infraspinatus muscle — one of four rotator cuff muscles, below spine of the scapula

Internal Rotation (IR) — rotate toward center of the body

Isometric contraction — muscle tightens but no motion occurs

-itis — inflammation

Kyphosis — natural curve in mid back

Lateral — toward the outside of the body

Lateral epicondylitis — "tennis elbow," tendonitis on the outside of the elbow

Ligament — tissue that connects bone to bone

Lordosis — natural curve in the low back and neck

Lower extremity — leg

Lumbar — low back, five lumbar vertebrae

Lymph drainage — very light manual therapy technique

Massage/manual therapy — hands-on technique

Medial — toward the center of the body

Medial epicondylitis — "golfer's elbow," tendonitis on the inside of the elbow

Meniscus — medial and lateral C-shaped cartilage in the knee, provides cushioning between femur and tibia

Musculoskeletal — muscle, bones, and joints

Myofascial release — deep massage technique affecting muscle (myo) and fascia (thick connective tissue)

Orthopedic — involving bones, joints, and muscles

Orthotic — shoe insert

Osteoarthritis — degenerative joint disease, DJD

Osteoporosis — loss of bone density

Patella — knee cap

Plantar fasciitis — inflammation of thick tissue on bottom of foot

Prone — lie on stomach

Psoas muscle — attaches to the front of the low back vertebrae and runs through the groin to front of hip

Radius — forearm bone next to thumb

Retrograde massage — assisting/pushing fluid out of a swollen area, toward the heart, to be reabsorbed by the body

R.I.C.E. — rest, ice, compression, elevation

Rice sock — two pounds of uncooked rice in long sock, tie/sew to close

ROM — range of motion

Rotator cuff — four shoulder muscles:

   Supraspinatus — above spine of the scapula

   Infraspinatus — below spine of the scapula

   Teres minor — below infraspinatus

   Subscapularis — under the shoulder blade

Sacro-iliac joint (SIJ) — connects sacrum to pelvis (ilium)

Sacrum — triangle bone at base of the spine

Scapula — shoulder blade

Soleus — a calf muscle, stretch with knee slightly bent

Spinal cord — the nerves connecting the body and brain

Spine — back bones, or ridge of bone on shoulder blade

Spine of the scapula — ridge of bone on shoulder blade

Sprain — injury to a ligament that connects bone to bone

Stenosis — narrowing

Sternum — breast bone

Strain — injury to muscle or tendon

Subscapularis muscle — one of four rotator cuff muscles, under the shoulder blade

Supraspinatus muscle — one of four rotator cuff muscles, above the spine of the scapula

Synovial fluid — fluid in joints

Tendon — tissues that connect a muscle to a bone

YOUR BODY BOOK

Tendonitis — inflammation of a tendon

"Tennis elbow" — lateral epicondylitis, tendonitis on the outside of the elbow

TENS or **TNS** — transcutaneous electrical nerve stimulation; used to relieve pain

Teres minor muscle — one of four rotator cuff muscles, below the infraspinatus on the shoulder blade

Tibia — shin bone on lower leg, with fibula

Thoracic — mid back, 12 thoracic vertebrae

Thoracic Outlet Syndrome (TOS) — compression of nerves, arteries, and/or veins, in collar bone area, causing arm symptoms

TMJ-Temporomandibular joint — jaw joint

Trigger point — a tight tender area in a muscle; when pressed, it sends symptoms to other parts of the body

Ulna — forearm bone next to little finger

Upper extremity — arm

Vasoconstriction — closing of vessels that *decreases* blood flow

Vasodilation — opening of vessels that *increases* blood flow

Vertebra — single back bone

Vertebrae — multiple back bones

Whiplash — quick snapping motion

WFL — within *functional* limits, enough to get by, usually 80 % of normal motion and/or strength

WNL — within *normal* limits, 80-100% of normal motion and/or strength

Index

Acetabulum, hip socket, 40
Acid, 64, 67, 77, 93-94, 100
Acromion, 16-17
Acupressure, 13, 73
Acute, 18, 24, 30, 32, 55, 62, 64
ADLs, Activities of Daily Living, 93, 99
Aerobic, 93, 99
Air, atmospheric pressure, 8, 89-90
Alcohol slush ice pack, 64, **66**
Align, 18, 48
Aligned, 6, 43, 82
Alignment, 5, 18, 31, 39-40, 45, 88, 93
"All or none," 100
Ankle, **42-43**, 44, 54, 65, 119
Anti-inflammatory, 64, 81
Arm, upper extremity, 7, 15-26, 34, 38, 47, 51, 57-58, 60, 68,
    71-72, 82-84, 91, 108-111, 113, 117
Arthritis, 6, 40, 44, 49-**50**
Arteries, 25-26, 43
Axilla, arm pit, 18, 26, 71
Back, ix, 15, 25, 28-40, 43-44, 50, 57-58, 67-72, 77, 80, 82,
    84, 87, 90, 104, 112-119
        Pain, 25, 27-**31,** 37, 39, 43, 57, 68-69, 80, 87
        Pain relief, 30-**32,** 33, 35-37, 69-72, 90, 112-116
        Exercises, **33-38**, 104, **112-117**
Back bends, 29, **36**, 69, 90, **115**
Balance, 6, 12, 38, 42, 54, 82, **85**-88, 103, 117
Barometer, 89
Bladder, loss of control, 32, 91
Blood clot, 90
Body mechanics, 31, **84**
Body pillow, 72
Body's rules, **101**
Bone spur, 6, 16, 50
Bowel, loss of control, 32, 91
Brain, 7, 11, 59-61, 71, 73, 77-78, 80, 91, 97, 99, 107

Breast bone, sternum, 15, 27
Bridge exercise, **34**, 38, **113**, 117
Bursa, 16, 49, 51
Bursitis, 16, 40, 49, **51**
Buttock, 32-34, 37, 39-40, 43, 57, 70, 112-113, 116
Calcium, 16, 79, 87
Calf muscles stretching exercise, 42, **44**, 104, **119**
Centralized symptoms, 32, 35, 114
Cerebral spinal fluid, 73
Certified Hand Therapist, CHT, 24
Cervical spine, neck, ix, xi, 3-4, **6-14**, 15, 19, 25-27, 50, 57-58,
    67-68, 70, 72, 80, 82, 84, 87, 90, 104, 106-107
        Care, **9**
        Pain, **12-13**
        Stretching exercises, **10-11**, 104, **106-107**
        Traction, 12, **14**
        Whiplash, 4, **8**
"Chicken wings" shoulder exercise, **21**, **109**
Chin tuck, **10**, 13, 69, 82, 84, **106**
Chondromalacia, 41
Chronic, 62, 67
Clavicle, collar bone, 15, 26
Closed-chain strengthening exercise, 104, 120
Clunking, **53**
Coccyx, tail bone, 28
Cold, 48, 58-66
Collagen, 92
Collar bone, clavicle, 15, 26
Compression fracture of the spine, 87
Core muscles strengthening, 31, 38, 93, 117
Cranial Sacral Therapy, **73**
Crepitation, 5, **53**, 105, 120
Cross-fiber massage, friction massage, **74**
Curl-up, crunch exercise, **34**, 38, **113**, 117
DDD, degenerative disc disease, 6, 28, 30
Disc, 6-7, 28-31, 35, 57, 68, 77, 80, 84, 87, 114
      In the jaw, TMJ, 4-5
      Injuries, **29**-30, 35
DJD, degenerative joint disease, 6, 28, 40, 50

YOUR BODY BOOK 131

Elbow, **24**, 50, 52, 65

Electrical stimulation and/or TENS, 17, 59-60, 80

Elevation, 89-90

Emergency, 32, **91**

"ER-at-side" shoulder exercise, **20, 23, 108, 111**

Exercise, 18, 47-48, 50, 52, 54, 77, 86, 89, 92, 94, 96, **97, 99**, 102
    Myths, **100**

Exercises, xi, 4-5, 9-11, 19-23, 29-30, 33-38, 40-43, 69, 80, 87, 90, 99, 103, **104-120**

Extension of the back, 29, **35-36**, 104, **114-115**

External Rotation, ER, of the shoulder, 19-**20, 23, 108, 111**

Facet, 7-8, 31

Fascia, 44, 73

Fear, xiii, **95**

Feet, 43-**44**, 50, 119

Femur, 40-41

Fibula, 41

Flexible, 6, 9, 40, 48, 50, 63, 74, **86**-88, 92, 97, 99-100, 103, 118-119

Flexion, 10, 19, 22, 30, 33-34, 37, 104, 106, 110, 112-113, 116

FIDA, frequency, intensity, duration, area, 32, 96

Foam roll, 27, 38, 117

Foramen, 7

Fracture, 87, 92

Friction massage, cross-fiber massage, **74**

Gastrocnemius calf muscle, 42-44, 104, 119

Gel, lotion, 59-61, 80, 93

Genetic, inherited, 44, 50, 86

"Golfer's elbow," medial epicondylitis, **24**

Goop, **61**

"Goose necking," 13, 68

Groin, 31, 37, 39-**40**

Grinding, 4-5, 41, **53**, 85, 105

Hamstrings stretching, 104, **118**

Hand, 14, 16, 20-22, **24**, 36, 44, 50, 73, 78, 86, 108-110, 115

Head, ix, xi, 1, 3-4, 6-7, 9-14, 34, 36, 68-70, 73, 82, 84, 104, 106-107, 113, 115, 118

Headache, **3**, 6, 9, 12, 68, 79

Health history/journal, 80, 94, **96**

132   YOUR BODY BOOK

Heat, 3, 9, 12, 18, 24, 31-32, 42, 54-55, 59-63, **67**, 72, 80, 89-90, 93, 95

Hip, 31-32, 34, 37, 39-**40**, 43-44, 50-51, 53, 57, 71-72, 84, 90, 104, 113, 116

    Exercises, 33-34, 36-37, 104, 112-113, 115-116

Hormonal, 80, 86, **88**

Hot, 12, 16-18, 27, 32, 42, 48-49, 58-63, 67

Humerus, 15-16

"Hurt so good," 3, 13, 18, 73

Ice, 3, 8-9, 12, 16-18, 24, 27, 31-32, 42, 44, 48-49, 51-52, 54-55, 59, **61-66**, 80-81, 90, 93, 95

    Alcohol slush pack, 64, **66**

    Ice massage, 52, 64-**65**

    Ice pack, 64-**66**

    R.I.C.E., rest, ice, compress, elevate, 42, 64-**65**

Ilio-tibial band, ITB, 40

Ilium, 39

Impingement, 7, **16**, 20

Inflamed, 7, 16, 31, 48, 62-63

Inflammation, 6, 24, 31, 44, **48-49**, 50-54, 62, 77

Infraspinatus muscle, 17

Inherited, genetic, 44, 50, 86

Internal Rotation, IR, of the shoulder, 19, **21**, **109**

Isometric, 90, 100

"It hurts so good," 3, 13, 18, 73

-*itis*, inflammation, 24, **49**

Jaw, TMJ, temporomandibular joint, **4-5**, 69, 104-105

Joint, xi, 1, 4-9, 15, 19, 28, 31, 33, 37, 39-41, 43, 45, 49-51, 53-54, 57-58, 68, 72, 77, 86, 88-89, 92, 99, 105, 116

Journal/health history, 80, 94, **96**

Knee, ix, 32-34, 37, **41**, 43-44, 47, 50, 53, 60, 69-72, 80, 82-83, 85-86, 90, 104, 112-113, 116, 118-120

    Bend, small squat, 53, 85, 90, 104, **120**

    Cap, patella, 41, 47, 85

    Exercises, **33-34**, **37**, 104, **112-113**, **116**, **118-120**

    Prone knee flexion exercise, **37**, 104, **116**

Knee-to-chest exercise, 30, **33**, 40, 80, **112**

Lateral, 24, 41, 52

Lateral epicondylitis, "tennis elbow," **24**, 52

YOUR BODY BOOK   133

Leg, lower extremity, ix, 32-44, 47, 50, 56-58, 70, 72, 82-85,
    91, 112-120
Ligament, 8, 41-43, 53-54, 74, 80, 82, 86, 88, 92
Log roll, 83
Lotion, gel, 59-61, 80, 93
Low back, lumbar spine, **28-38**, 58, 67, 69, 80, 82, 87, 112-117
    Pain, **31**
    Pain relief, **32**
    Exercises, **33-38**, 104, **112-117**
Lower extremity, leg, ix, 32-44, 47, 50, 56-58, 70, 72, 82-85,
    91, 112-120
Lumbar, see low back
Lymph, 48, 63, 73, 92
Massage, manual therapy, 3, 12-13, 18, 43, 48, 52, 59, 64-65,
    73-74, 77, 92
Medial, 24, 41
Medial epicondylitis, "golfer's elbow," 24
Medication, 17, **81**, 87, 93-96
Men, 21, 29, 86, 103
Meniscus, cartilage in the knee, 41
Midback, thoracic spine, **25**, 27, 87
"More is better," 100
Morning stiffness, 8, 29, 54
Muscle spasm, 8-9, 13-14, 19, 32, 56, 62, 64, 68, 70
Musculoskeletal, xi, 45
Myofascial release, 73
Neck, cervical spine, ix, xi, 3-4, **6-14**, 15, 19, 25-27, 50, 57-58,
    67-68, 70, 72, 80, 82, 84, 87, 90, 104, 106-107
    Care, **9**
    "Goose necking," 13, 68
    Pain, **12-13**
    Stretching exercises, **10-11**, 104, **106-107**
    Traction, 12, **14**
    Whiplash, 4, **8**
Nerve, 7, 25-26, 29-31, 35, 43, 58-59, 61, 68, 73, 88, 91-92, 114
"No pain, no gain," 100
Nutrition, 5, 8, 48-49, 63-64, 67, 73, **77-79**, 86, 93, 96, 99
On the road again, **90**
Orthopedic, xi, 16-17, 92, 137

Orthotic, 44
Osteoarthritis, 50
Osteoporosis, 87
Pain, **56-61**
    Pain control, **59**
Patella, knee cap, 41, 47, 85
Pectoralis major/minor muscles, 20, 26, 108
Pelvic tilt, 30, **33**, 38, 69, 80, 82, **112**, 117
Pelvis, 32, 35, **39**-40, 43-44, 57, 69, 71-72, 82, 114
Perspective, **92**
Pillow, 9, 12, 15, 17, 26, 32, 68, 70-**72**, 80, 84, 93
Plantar fasciitis, 44
Popping, 4, **53**, 85
Position, 4, 6-7, 12-13, 16, 18, 22, 24-27, 29, 31-32, 35, 68-70,
    82-84, 90, 110, 114
Positional release, 70
Positioning, 7, 9, 13, 31, 59, **68-70**, 80, 93, 95
    For pain relief, **70**
Posture, 6-7, 9, 12-**13**, 18-19, 24-26, 31, 50, **68-69**, **82**, 86-87
Prone, 35, 37, 104, 114, 116
Prone-on-elbows, 35, 114
Prone knee flexion exercise, **37**, 104, **116**
Press-up exercise, 35, 114
Psoas muscle, 31, 37, 40
Push-up exercise, 23, 104, 111, **120**
Range of motion, ROM, 18, 54-55, 93
Retrograde massage, 73
Rheumatoid arthritis, 50
Rib, 15, 17, 25, **27**, 57
    First, 25, 27
R.I.C.E., rest, ice, compress, elevate, 42, 64-**65**
Rice sock, 9-**12**, 18, 66-**67**, 69-70, 72, 90, 106-107
ROM, range of motion, 18, 54-55, 93
Rotator cuff injury, **17**
Rotator cuff muscles, 17, 23, 111
        Supraspinatus, 17
        Infraspinatus, 17
        Teres minor, 17
        Subscapularis, 17, 20, 108

YOUR BODY BOOK

Sacro-iliac joint, SIJ, 31, 39-40, 57, 88

Sacrum, 28, 39

Scapula, shoulder blade, 15-17, 20-21, 27, 108-109

Scar tissue, 48, 74, 92

Shoulder, 7, 10-11, 13, **15-23**, 25-27, 51, 53, 57-58, 60, 69, 71-72, 80, 82, 90, 104, 106-111

    Blade, 15-17, 20-21, 27, 108-109

    Care, **18**

    Exercises, **19-23**, 90, 104, **108-111**

    Impingement, **16**

    Rotator cuff injury, **17**

Shorter with age, 30, 77, **87**

SIJ, sacro-iliac joint, 31, 39-40, 57, 88

Sit-to-stand, 83

Skin lift/roll, 74

Sleep, 7, 15, 26, 29, 32, 67, 71, 77, **80**-81, 87-88, 92-96, 99

Small squat, knee bend, 53, 85, 90, 104, **120**

Snapping, **53**

Soleus, calf muscle, 42-44, 104, 119

Spinal cord, 7, 73, 91

Spine, **6**-7, **25**, 27-**28**, 30, 33, 39, 72, 87, 91

Spine of the scapula, 17

Sprain, 41-42, **54**, 65

Stenosis, **30**

Sternum, breast bone, 15, 27

"Stick-em-up" shoulder exercise, 20, 108

Stiff, 7-9, 29, 32, 42-43, 48, 54-55, 62, 67, 77, 80, 86, 89-90

Strain, 12, 32, 50, **55**, 71-72, 84, 90

Strain-Counterstrain, 70

Stress, 50, 68, 72, 80, 84, 90, **94**-96, 99

Stretching rules, **9**, 52, **102**

Strengthening rules, 52, **102**

Subscapularis muscle, 17, 20, 108

Supraspinatus muscle, 17

Swedish massage, 73

Swelling, xi, 7-9, 16, 24, 31, 41-43, 45, 47-48, 51-52, 54-56, 62, 64, 73-74, 77, 81, 90, 92-93

Tail bone, coccyx, 28

Teeth, 4-5, 68-69

136   YOUR BODY BOOK

Tendon, 24, 43, 49, 52-53, 55, 74, 92
Tendonitis, 24, 49, **52**
Tennis ball, 3, 27
"Tennis elbow," lateral epicondylitis, 24, 52
TENS, TNS, transcutaneous electrical nerve stimulation, 17, **60**, 80
Teres minor muscle, 17
Therapy ball, 27, 38, 117
Thoracic, mid back, **25**, 27, 87
Thoracic Outlet Syndrome, TOS, **26**
Tibia, 41
Time to heal, 31, 43, **92**, 95
TMJ, temporomandibular joint, jaw, **4-5**, 69, 104-105
       Exercises, **5**, 104-**105**
       Resting position, 4
Towel, 9-12, 14-15, 29, 32, 36, 66, 71-72, 84, 106-107, 115
Toxin, 48, 64, 67, 77-78, 93-94
Traction, 12, **14**-15
Trigger point, 40, **58**
Trigger point release, 73
Upper extremity, arm, 7, 15-26, 34, 38, 47, 51, 57-58, 60, 68,
       71-72, 82-84, 91, 108-111, 113, 117
Vasoconstrict, 48-49, 63-64
Vasodilate, 48-49, 63-64, 67
Veins, 25-26, 43
Vertebra, 6-7, 10, 25, 27-31, 37, 77, 87, 106
Walking when injured, **47**
Water, 40, 44, 50, 64-66, 70, **77**-78, 87-88, 103
Weak, 6-7, 18, 68, 87, 91
Weather, 8, 43, **89**-90
Whiplash, 4, **8**
Women, 21, 86, **88**, 103
Wrist, **24**, 65

About The Author

Photo by José Marroquín

Doranne Long, PT, MS has been a physical therapist since 1981. She received a Bachelor of Science in Physical Therapy from the University of Puget Sound, in Tacoma, Washington. In 1988, she completed a Master of Science in Physical Therapy at Massachusetts General Hospital Institute of Health Professions, in Boston.

She specializes as an orthopedic manual physical therapist and recognizes how vital it is to care for ourselves physically as well as mentally, emotionally, and spiritually. She is passionate about empowering people, through education, to successfully manage their health.

The material in this book is based on the author's knowledge and practice and is intended to help the general public. Consult health care professionals with specific medical conditions.

Contact Information

Doranne Long, PT, MS

D's TheraP LLC

P.O. Box 5735, Grants Pass, OR 97527

Doranne@yourbodybook.com

www.YourBodyBook.com